The 20 British Prime Ministers
of the 20th century

My parents Maureen Elizabeth Morgan and Donald Edward Morgan are children of the MacDonald years. This book is dedicated to them.

MacDonald

KEVIN MORGAN

HAUS PUBLISHING · LONDON

First published in Great Britain in 2006 by
Haus Publishing Limited
70 Cadogan Court, London SW1X 9AH

Reprinted in 2018

Copyright © Kevin Morgan, 2006

A CIP catalogue record for this book is available from the British Library

ISBN 978-1-904950-61-5

Designed by BrillDesign
Typeset in Garamond 3 by MacGuru Ltd

Printed in the United Kingdom

Cover over illustration: John Holder

Contents

Introduction: A Hybrid Ancestry

Keir Hardie, Arthur Henderson and Ramsay MacDonald, perhaps the three principal architects of the Labour Party, had one thing apart from politics in common: all three of them were illegitimate. Though this was not as remarkable as some Victorian stereotypes suggest, it might have seemed almost a symbol of Labour's outsider status had only the information been publicly known. What the three had in common, however, they may not even have known themselves. For both Hardie and Henderson, the details of their births awaited the attentions of biographers long after their deaths, and the possible stigma of bastardy had no obvious effect on their public careers. MacDonald's case was very different. Although he alone of the three achieved the country's highest office, in 1924, his illegitimacy had by this time been exposed by the yellow press in the fever of the First World War. It was an experience foreshadowing the excesses of our own times. 'No wonder the Moray Golf Club, of which he is a member, requests him to resign', commented the poisonous sheet *John Bull*, which broke the story. 'What says the country, which is paying this man £400 a year to vilify and discredit it?'[1]

£400 was the salary paid MacDonald as one of the elected members for Leicester and Labour's most distinguished parliamentarian. The Moray Golf Club was a key social institution in MacDonald's home town of Lossiemouth on the

Moray Firth. The vilification of which he was accused was to have expressed misgivings about the war of the most studied moderation. Among supporters, the attack provoked a wave of sympathy and anger which only reinforced MacDonald's reputation for integrity in the face of adversity. Nevertheless, the 'country', in the shape of his Leicester constituents, delivered a devastating verdict in the post-war 'Khaki' election two years later. Defeated by a margin of more than three to one, MacDonald's rejection was emphatic even in the context of the general rout that occurred of internationalists and peace campaigners.

The impact that this had upon him can only be surmised. His daughter Ishbel, possibly the closest of his children to him, described his illegitimacy as the central influence on his life.[2] Godfrey Elton, a family friend and MacDonald's biographer, described how as a boy, provoked by an 'unforgivable remark', he threw a stone at a schoolmate that could have killed him.[3] *As far back as I can remember I had a grudge against the world rankling in me*, MacDonald himself recalled a few years later. *As a youngster I can remember I had one of the most violent tempers ever known …*[4] Called upon to clear up the details of his background for his intended wife's family, he also described his weariness at having to go over such matters again. *They have so often raised their heads when I felt happy. God knows, though, I have done penance for them.*[5] A tendency to self-dramatisation was one of his most marked characteristics. But then his illegitimacy perhaps was one of its causes.

MacDonald, more than most of us, was a creature of paradox. A plausible assessment is that he is the most difficult of all 20th-century prime ministers to make sense of.[6] He was a radical with conservative tastes and instincts; a socialist ideologue who never broke with Liberalism; a metropolitan intriguer, who escaped his origins but kept returning to them; and a remorseless careerist who, in the 1914–18 war, appeared to wreck his every prospect for a point of principle. Above all, he was a figurehead for the new mass democracy who never really trusted it, and both within and against it upheld the necessity of reform as the precondition of stability. Elton, who was an admirer, attributed his dualism to the mixing of Highland and Lowland blood. His fellow socialist Beatrice Webb, who was not, saw only the calculated insincerity of a poseur.

I shall be a more solitary figure than ever – a mule, in short, with a hybrid ancestry and no possible posterity.

MACDONALD

In truth, MacDonald was not a born aristocrat, as Webb suggested, but an outsider whose greatest ambition and insecurity was his craving for acceptance and recognition. Perhaps the MacDonald who became notorious for consorting with duchesses was quietly avenging himself on schoolboy insults or on the committee of the Moray Golf Club. Returning to Lossiemouth, as he so often did, may have reminded him not just of where he had come from, but of how far he had gone. Did it also sometimes remind him of things that were lost in getting there? Cynics said that his ambition was to stand at the top of the great staircase of Londonderry House, where the grandest receptions of the Tory establishment took place. When he achieved this ambition, as head of a basically Conservative government, he allowed himself the bitter reflection: *I shall be a more solitary figure than ever – a mule, in short, with a hybrid ancestry and no possible posterity.*[7] The metaphor is perfect. We need to begin the journey with his hybrid ancestry.

Part One

THE LIFE

MacDonald's mother, Anne Ramsay, was not quite the 'Scotch servant girl' that *John Bull* alleged. Nor was the 'Scottish peasant parents' of Labour accounts entirely accurate either.[1] Though family conditions were hard and Anne had certainly worked as a servant, she is described by MacDonald's official biographer, David Marquand, as a skilled seamstress. According to one Lossiemouth old-timer, she was also so outspoken in her radicalism that during the South African War of 1900–2 she was burned in effigy.[2] Moreover, though MacDonald lacked a father, his mother was helped in bringing him up by his grandmother, Bella Ramsay, who was an ardent churchgoer with a strong sense of her social standing. It is Bella who is said to have ruled out MacDonald's genuine peasant father as a marriage partner for her daughter. It was also in Bella's home that the family lived, and where her stock of Celtic folklore and mysticism is said to have fed the brooding, romantic side of the youngster's character.[3] Brought up as an only child in a tiny 'but and ben' – a two-roomed Scottish cottage – MacDonald went without many things. He did not, however, want attention, nor a sense of his own calling to a higher station.

Nor, for one of such humble circumstances, did he entirely lack an education. A beneficiary of the greater opportunities enjoyed by the able but disadvantaged child in Scotland, MacDonald was to pay warm tribute to the master (or dominie) at the parish school he attended at nearby Drainie. *The machinery*, he wrote, *was as old as Knox; the education was the best ever given to the sons and daughters of men.*[4] The formal schooling was more than adequate. More important still were the readings to which the dominie introduced his gifted pupil, including such staples for awakening late Victorian minds as Carlyle and Ruskin. Briefly MacDonald is said to have begun work as a farm labourer. Whether derived from that experience, or from the dominie's editions of Henry David Thoreau, a sense of the rugged independence of such work was to have an important influence on MacDonald's wider social philosophy. Nevertheless, with his passionate appetite for learning it was inevitable that he should take up the opportunity of continuing at Drainie as a pupil teacher when it was offered him. Already while still in his teens, his intellectual interests began to flourish. In 1883 he set up a Lossiemouth Field Club and produced a cyclostyled magazine for it. He also took part in the debates of the local Mutual Improvement Society. The literary and oratorical skills on which he was to make his national reputation were first honed and tested in this Scottish fishing village.

For any young man with ambitions, however, Lossiemouth was not big enough to contain them. Scouring the situations vacant column in the *Scotsman*, in 1885, at the age of 19, MacDonald was taken on as assistant to a Bristol clergyman who was setting up a boys' and young men's guild. Though he remained in Bristol barely six months, he had no intention now of returning permanently to Lossiemouth and early the following year made what turned out to be the permanent move to London. Lossiemouth would remain a crucial point of reference for MacDonald and even as Prime Minister he would several times a year retreat to the home he had built there for his mother. Paradoxically, however, that depended on his having made good in the capital. For the time being, some 550 miles from home, the wrench must have seemed complete.

MacDonald did not need London to introduce him to radicalism. Already in Lossiemouth, the writers with whom he became familiar included the American Henry George, whose panacea of the land tax had a special resonance in the Scottish highlands. MacDonald is also said to have seen the *Christian Socialist* of J L Joynes, who in 1883 had helped set up a Land Reform Union on Georgeite lines. *The whole of my part of Scotland was Radical*, he later wrote, *and we seemed to have been born with the democratic spirit strongly developed in us.*[5] Nevertheless, if radicalism was pervasive, the socialism he would later embrace was at this point still an esoteric creed, barely established as a political movement. MacDonald could have spent a long time on the Moray coast without making any direct acquaintance with it. Even in Bristol, one of its main provincial centres, he is said to have had recourse to a policeman to help seek it out.[6] The socialism of the Independent Labour Party (ILP), with which he was to be so intimately associated, is typically regarded as having grown 'from the bottom up', in the shadowy provinces. MacDonald's distinctiveness was that almost from the start it was associated with the bustle and opportunity of the capital.

Already in Bristol he had become active in the Marxist Social Democratic Federation (SDF). Curiously, that prefigured Ernest Bevin, another of Labour's pantheon of illegitimates and a native of the city. There, however, the

> *The whole of my part of Scotland was Radical, and we seemed to have been born with the democratic spirit strongly developed in us.*
>
> MACDONALD

resemblance between them ends, and at the climacteric of MacDonald's career in 1931 he and Bevin seemed to personify almost diametrically opposed conceptions of the labour movement. Where Bevin remained active in the local industrial movement, only finally emerging into Labour politics as secretary of Britain's largest trade union, MacDonald's move to the capital introduced him to a new and kaleidoscopic world of meetings, campaigns, discussion circles, publications – and career opportunities. Socialism was important, but it was only a part of what London had to offer. Educationally, MacDonald discovered the Guildhall Library, the Birkbeck Institute and the British Museum reading room. Politically, he was to be attracted by a range of different organisations, from the Scottish Home Rule Association to the 'ethical' movement and the Fellowship of the New Life. And professionally, he was to make his first fateful connections on the radical wing of the Liberal Party.

All this was not untypical of *fin-de-siècle* London. On arriving in the capital MacDonald was active in a short-lived moderate SDF breakaway called the Socialist Union. Nevertheless, though London was a centre for the SDF and for the militant 'New Unionism' of dockers and other unskilled workers, the tradition of independent Labour politics was never to be as strong here as in the provinces. Instead, 'constructive' socialism was dominated by the idea of a broader progressivism, actively sponsored by the very much London-based Fabian Society. Founded in 1884 and still existing today, the early Fabian Society is usually seen as the vehicle of a new social stratum, or *nouvelle couche sociale*, of the talented but propertyless salariat. Drawn towards the expanding commercial and professional opportunities of the imperial metropolis, these typically lacked advantages of birth or education. Nevertheless, they found the doors of the old class society just sufficiently ajar to feed ambitions of a new social order in which their talents would be utilised and rewarded, if only in status. Though formally speaking Mac-Donald's relationship with the Fabian Society was to become somewhat fraught, he remained in many respects typical of this *nouvelle couche sociale*. Even as he became drawn into independent Labour politics, he was also to show a strong and persistent tendency towards the cross-party conceptions of the Fabians.

For his first year or two in London, MacDonald made an exiguous living in dead-end clerical jobs. As he described it many years later, *I went every morning to the City in the wake of the monarchs of finance; scrawled and scribbled and added and subtracted all day ... and felt that I was one of those undistinguished ants who would be lucky if they continued by honest and effective service to earn a latch key and daily bread.*[7] Desperate for an escape route, or simply frustrated by his work, he nurtured hopes of obtaining a science scholarship at South Kensington and pursued his political and educational commitments so intensely as to bring him to the point of breakdown.

It was thus one of the key moments in his career when in 1888 MacDonald secured a position that for the first time promised to satisfy both his material and his emotional needs. This was as secretary to the radical politician Thomas Lough, who at this time was Liberal candidate for West Islington, organising secretary of the Home Rule Union and well connected with metropolitan Liberal circles. 'Secretary-ships were important stepping-stones in MacDonald's career', Elton notes laconically; and Lough's produced the 'startling evolution' of a 'starving young Scottish peasant' into 'the arresting young politician who argued with the Fabians in their prosperous drawing rooms, and lunched with success-ful journalists in Fleet Street'.[8] Ironically, it was also through these London connections that MacDonald enjoyed his first important electoral experience nearer to home, assisting the radical Seymour Keay in a parliamentary by-election at Moray and Nairn. Through all the vicissitudes that were to follow, MacDonald was henceforth to make his way through his facility with words, whether as journalist or politician. In 1892, he left Lough's employment, not, it appears, because of any political falling out, but because he now felt either assured or frustrated enough to embark on a career as a freelance journalist and lecturer. Positioned on the radical fringe of Gissing's *New Grub Street*, it provided at first only a tenuous income. It did, however, allow him a sense of independence and a space in which he could dream of making his own mark.

A political career, in the form of a parliamentary seat, thus began to loom larger on MacDonald's horizons while at the same time remaining entirely beyond his reach. MacDonald was later to observe how evident it was to the social reformer *how powerful the letter, the nod, the wink of a Member of Parliament was.*[9] Having worked so hard to get Keay and Lough into Parliament, perhaps he pondered what better qualifications they had for such work than he.

George Gissing (1857–1903) published his first novel *Workers in the Dawn* in 1880. Its hero, based in many respects on Gissing himself, is made wretched by his marriage to an unlettered prostitute whose manners and morals he had sought to improve. Torn between self-interest and a misconceived altruism, he dies by throwing himself off the Niagara Falls. Gissing's most famous novel was *New Grub Street* (1891). It provides a memorable picture of the toils of literary hackwork with which MacDonald himself was familiar. Though posthumously acclaimed by writers like George Orwell, Gissing himself met with little literary success during his own lifetime.

It was the disappointment of any such expectations in the Liberal Party that underlay his adoption of the cause of independent Labour politics in the summer of 1894. Far away from London, the ILP's formation in Bradford the previous year had signalled a wider determination to sweep away such obstacles. The ILP's support was nevertheless concentrated mainly in the north, and MacDonald remained hopeful of achieving a Liberal candidacy with the support of the TUC-sponsored Labour Electoral Association. It was only the dashing of these hopes, first in Dover and then in Southampton, that decided him to join the ILP in July 1894. He announced his adhesion in a letter to the ILP's founder and chief inspiration, Keir Hardie:

My dear Hardie, I am now making personal application for membership of the ILP. I have stuck to the Liberals up to now, hoping that they might do something to justify the trust that we had put in them... .

Between you and me there was never any dispute as to object. What I could not quite accept was your methods. I have changed my opinion. Liberalism, and more particularly local Liberal Associations, have definitely declared against Labour, and so I must accept the facts of the situation and candidly admit that the prophecies of the ILP relating to Liberalism have been amply justified. The time for conciliation has gone by ... [10]

Though clearly expressing MacDonald's personal sense of frustration, there is little sign here of any major ideological cleavage. On the other hand, perhaps the same might have been said about Hardie's repudiation of the Liberal caucus just a few years earlier. The combination of a robust organisational rivalry with profound ideological indebtedness was to characterise MacDonald's relations with Liberalism almost throughout his career.

Its contradictory character can be detected from the start.

In the 1895 election MacDonald fought his first parliamentary campaign as an independent Labour candidate in the two-member constituency of Southampton. Gaining fewer than 1,000 votes and finishing at the bottom of the poll, his one achievement appears to have been to have deprived a sympathetic Liberal of his seat – or at least to appear to have done so. Certainly, when MacDonald returned to Lossiemouth after the election, he found his fellow villagers were all turned keen politicians and *swearing at me for having knocked out a 'Radigal'.*[11] MacDonald himself, at least to Liberal friends, blamed much on the leadership of Hardie, who *by his own incapacity lost his seat and none of us – being scapegoats – got it ...*[12] When almost immediately one of the successful Southampton candidates was unseated over alleged electoral malpractices, MacDonald sanctioned a secret trade-off in which the ILP's abstention in the resulting by-election would ensure the Liberals only contesting one of the seats in the next general election. Already on his first venture into electoral politics, MacDonald was thinking on the lines of the national electoral pact that he would negotiate with the Liberals in 1903. In Southampton, when in 1897 he spent a night *en route* for the USA with the local Liberal chief rather than his ILP supporters, the suggestion was made that he take his candidacy elsewhere.[13]

Though the ILP was to become identified as MacDonald's political home, his political outlook was thus at least as profoundly shaped by the Fabian political environment of the capital. To some extent this was obscured by his antagonism towards Sidney and Beatrice Webb, who then and long afterwards were the pre-eminent Fabians. In 1896 he clashed sharply with the Webbs over the diverting of a Fabian legacy into the establishment of the London School of Economics (LSE). Four years later he broke with the society over its refusal to condemn the South African war, and henceforth consistently disparaged its lack of genuine influence over the labour movement. Nevertheless, MacDonald had joined the Fabian Society as early as 1886, had made his first real acquaintance with Britain's industrial districts as a Fabian lecturer in 1892 and from 1894 to 1900 had been a member of the society's executive. Seduced by the proximity of Britain's social and political elites, his own career, like theirs was guided by the Fabian watchwords of 'permeation' – working through established channels of influence – and cross-class collaboration.

To appreciate the complexities of his position the combative election he fought in Southampton needs to be balanced with his simultaneous involvement in the consensus-building of the Rainbow Circle. Taking its name from a tavern in Fleet Street, the Rainbow Circle was conceived in 1894 as a space for the cross-party progressivism that flourished in the capital and yet seemed threatened by the cleavages of the party. To some extent MacDonald's involvement was the fortuitous result of his availability for such London-based initiatives. On the other hand, London was not an accident in his life; it was not only where his career and political outlook were moulded, but where he had chosen to have them moulded and where he found the opportunities most congenial. When a journal, the *Progressive Review*, was launched in 1896 to promote the same political objects, MacDonald again was heavily involved – as usual as its secretary. The journal lasted less than a year, but the Rainbow Circle continued meeting until after the war and MacDonald was an assiduous attender and paper-giver. Tellingly, he was the only prominent ILPer to be associated with it.

Chapter 2: Marriage and Lincoln's Inn Fields: 1896–1900

Late Victorian London was like a magnet to gifted young men looking to make their way. This was the world of the Dubliner Bernard Shaw, prolific in the generation of novels, Fabian tracts and publishers' rejection slips. It was the world too of the young H G Wells, torn between literary ambitions and a hunger for a scientific education. It is a world most vividly evoked in the wonderful novels of George Gissing, Wakefield-born and a dropout from the future University of Manchester. Like all of these, MacDonald felt the pull of letters and the world of learning and it would be a mistake to regard him as devoted to politics to the exclusion of these other possibilities. Like Shaw, he was an habitué of the radical lecture circuit. Like Wells, he was intent on a scientific education until his breakdown in 1888. He also nurtured ambitions as a novelist, and an uncompleted manuscript of a novel survives. Handling the traumas of social caste with a Gissing-like morbidity and sensitivity, no doubt it displayed rather less of Gissing's literary skill. Nevertheless, there were many writers published who had less command of their trade than MacDonald, and it would be a mistake to regard him as preordained for a political career. MacDonald, like the others, wanted to make a name for himself; but, for better or worse, his career was never to show the total absorption in politics of some of his Labour colleagues.

In the achievement of his goals, his marriage played a role of quite fundamental importance. This too was characteristic of its time. In his unfinished novel, MacDonald had dwelt on the plight of a socialist journalist who, from a misplaced social conscience, married an unlettered servant girl before finding a truer companionship in the love of an emancipated schoolteacher. The theme seems highly derivative of Gissing's first novel *Workers in the Dawn*, published in 1880, even to the extent of its culmination in suicide. In Gissing's novel, however, it was the hero, torn between his contradictory sexual impulses, who was driven to suicide. In MacDonald's, on the other hand, it was the lovelorn servant girl who took her own life on the shores of the Moray Firth.

In real life too, what we must assume to be MacDonald's merely imagined experience of an ill-matched liaison of compassion left no obstacles to the more companionate marriage

H G Wells (1866–1946) was one of the founders of the modern science fiction genre with such books as *The Time Machine*, *The War of the Worlds*, *The Invisible Man* and *The Island of Dr Moreau*, all written before 1900 and which have been filmed more than once. He also explored the lives of 'ordinary men' in books such as *Kipps* and *The Adventures of Mr Polly*. He was a Fabian socialist, and a eager exponent of social reform. His later career was dominated by works of history and social comment.

he made in 1896 to Margaret Ethel Gladstone. Distantly related to the famous politician, Margaret was a religious-minded East London charity worker, four years MacDonald's junior, of the sort so easily drawn towards the new socialist ideas of the day. She also came of a lineage which seemingly fascinated MacDonald and in the tribute which he later penned this to her provided the pedigree to which he could not lay claim himself. Her great uncles, the engineer James Thomson and the scientist and inventor Lord Kelvin, he described as *amongst the elect of mankind*.[1] Her father, John Gladstone, was a distinguished chemist and a fellow of the Royal Society. He was also a Liberal in politics and tolerant if not approving of socialist views. The family home in Pembridge Square stood in *reposeful dignity*, shut off from the bustle of the nearby Bayswater Road, and to MacDonald exuded *that air of detached independence which surrounds the English middle-class home of substantial possessions*.[2] How different it was from MacDonald's own 'model' dwelling block off the Gray's Inn Road, with its *ugliness, squalor, dullness and noise*. MacDonald, as experience was to show, was abnormally sensitive to his environment and this to him was like the *city of dreadful night*.[3]

Nobody reading his later tribute to Margaret could doubt the bonds of affection that united them. Nevertheless, by outcome if not intent, marriage was also a form of mobility, either upward or downward depending on the circumstances. MacDonald's were obviously upwards, and his was one of a number of socialist romances providing a release from material cares as well as emotional ones. Just four years earlier, Sidney Webb, having made a similarly adventitious marriage to Beatrice Potter, gave up his job in the Civil Service and devoted himself full-time to politics. The following year, 1893, the ILPer John Bruce Glasier was to find a similar respite from poverty through his marriage to Katherine Conway. Glasier and MacDonald were to collaborate closely as part of the ILP's 'Big Four'. Webb was to sit in both of MacDonald's Cabinets. For all of them, fortune in love meant security and opportunity in politics, at a time when the proliferation of political functions found all too few socialists of their backgrounds able to devote to them the largely unpaid service on which they depended. More than that, as novels like *New Grub Street* suggested, marriage on any other terms could mean just further subordination to the treadmill of the office or literary hackwork.

It was MacDonald who talked Margaret out of the *Quixotic notion* of giving up her independent income. His own income was then barely £100 and he had no illusion that this provided an adequate basis for a life of public service. *Reduce your cost of life to a moral minimum, do service to society, hold the rest as a trustee to the community*, he urged her; *but if you knew what it was to have ideal plans for work, a conviction of the strength to carry them out at least to a valuable point and no breakfast, you would see the real immorality of neglecting to use the opportunities you have in life.*[4]

Plans for work, like the Fabian strategy of permeation, required a bridgehead at the heart of the establishment. It was thus that the newly-weds moved to a spacious flat at 3 Lincoln's Inn Fields, described by Pevsner as a six-storeyed monstrosity overshadowing London's oldest square. MacDonald as yet was insensitive to such nuances. Instead, his new address allowed him to position himself at the centre of political affairs even before he secured entry into Parliament a decade later. The LSE, whose foundation he had so resisted, was just around the corner. Fleet Street, the Rainbow Tavern, the LCC, the South Place Ethical Society, all were just a few minutes away, along with a plethora of societies and publishing offices. Forced to find his own accommodation a few years later, Hardie too found a flat just a stone's-throw away. As if expressive of their very different styles of politics, Hardie's, however, was like a 'hermit's cell'.[5]

Possibly fearful of comparisons with the Webbs, whose own hospitality had been cruelly satirised by H G Wells, MacDonald denied that what he and Margaret established at their flat was a political salon. Nevertheless, this was precisely what it was. *Once every three weeks or so ... our rooms were crowded with men and women busy in the service of Labour and Socialism*, he remembered.

The shy recruit just arrived in London came to see those of whom he had heard much; the stranger from the ends of the earth, black, yellow, or white in colour, came as a guest; meetings were fixed up, plots may have been hatched ... it widened and widened until at last it stretched round the earth, and no mail came or went without bearing fibre of the bond which kept it together.[6]

MacDonald also made the most of the opportunities for travel which the couple's income allowed. Visits to North America, Australia and South Africa, and extensive travels in Europe, thus helped encourage the international sweep of interests which was to be one of his most striking political qualities. India, which he visited in 1910 and again, on a royal commission, in 1912–13, was to remain a preoccupation even as Prime Minister.

More than just a salon, the MacDonalds' home in Holborn provided a possible London office for a movement anchored in the provinces and yet aspiring to exercise influence in Westminster. One ILP collaborator described it as 'a cross between a library and an editorial office'.[7] MacDonald himself described it as *a workshop of social plan and effort*, suited to committee meetings and serviced by the unremunerated efforts of the MacDonalds themselves.[8] In 1906, for example, it was at Lincoln's Inn Fields that there took place the inaugural meeting of the Women's Labour League, effectively the women's section of the Labour Party. Presiding over its first conference, Margaret was also elected to the League's executive, for she

'It is rather appalling to think that you and I have to "live up" to the Webbs & Bosanquets!'

MARGARET MACDONALD

was a serious political campaigner in her own right. As she jocularly remarked of the two of best-known political partnerships of the day: 'It is rather appalling to think that you and I have to "live up" to the Webbs & Bosanquets!'[9]

Her husband, still more auspiciously, had drawn on the same advantages in carving out a key role in the foundation of the Labour Party itself. Taking shape in 1900 as the Labour Representation Committee (LRC), this new conception of the 'Labour Alliance' combined the exiguous resources of the early socialist movement with initially somewhat diffident commitments on the part of the trade unions. Until the threat to their legal immunities posed by the Taff Vale court judgement of 1901, many unions gave little thought to having their own independent representation in Parliament. Even then, and for many years afterwards, deep-seated commitment to sectional interests and forms of accountability constrained the development of a centralised party apparatus.

MacDonald's role was therefore crucial. At the LRC's founding conference on 27 February 1900, the first nominee as secretary was the Mancunian Fred Brocklehurst, who had more experience than MacDonald in both the ILP and in local socialist politics. Nevertheless, given the decision that the committee's offices be based in London, Brocklehurst felt compelled to withdraw on grounds of his commitments in Manchester. Instead, he proposed MacDonald, who as well as working without remuneration was able to provide the necessary office space in his own home. There were no other candidates, and the decision was taken essentially on grounds of economy and administrative convenience.

Nevertheless, there were also political implications of which even the delegates were possibly unaware. Within the ILP, MacDonald along with Hardie favoured contesting a relatively limited number of constituencies both to maximise effectiveness and to minimise conflict with the Liberals. As recently as the 1899 Trades Union Congress (TUC) which paved the way to the formation of the LRC, MacDonald had curiously referred to this as a victory for *the more extreme men* who favoured *continental methods of political work*.[10] In Woolwich, in the very month that the LRC was formed, he ran in harness with a Liberal as a 'Labour and Progressive' candidate for the LCC. The dissension that this provoked was to be echoed many times before 1914, as MacDonald sought simultaneously to establish a viable basis for Labour representation while steering it in the direction the 'progressive alliance'.

Chapter 3: From Pressure Group to Party: 1900–14

Between 1900 and 1914, MacDonald's contribution to the development of the Labour Party, as the LRC became known in 1906, was at least threefold. First, he functioned as a remarkably effective secretary, particularly in the early years of spadework when union sensitivities and old Liberal habits needed handling with both firmness and diplomacy. Secondly, he acted as a political strategist and negotiator, to some extent self-appointed, whose most significant accomplishment was the Gladstone-MacDonald electoral pact of 1903. Thirdly, from the time of his election to Parliament in 1906, and particularly after his election as chairman of the parliamentary party in February 1911, MacDonald was Labour's most accomplished performer in the House of Commons. Differences existed over the direction he gave the party. Some Liberals thought it merited a seat in the Cabinet. Some socialists would have been glad to see him go. But on its own terms this was arguably the most effective period in MacDonald's entire career.

MacDonald's first task as the LRC's secretary was to secure sufficient affiliations to place it on a viable financial basis. His second was to establish the LRC as a credible electoral threat at constituency level, whether directly at the polls or through the leverage which it could exercise over the Liberal

Party. He was assisted by the threat which the Taff Vale judgement posed to trade union funds, and immediately circulated the unions urging the need to secure redress through representation in Parliament. Nevertheless, it was due in no small measure to MacDonald's energy and persistence that such effective use was made of these circumstances. On its formation the LRC's affiliated trade union membership had stood at just 187,000. By 1906 it had reached nearly a million. With the affiliation of the miners in 1908, the figure increased by nearly half as much again; and in 1912 the party achieved its peak pre-war membership of 1.9 million. By this time, there were also local Labour organisations in nearly 150 constituencies. As a consequence of its success, in March 1904 the LRC at last removed itself to public premises from the room it occupied in the MacDonalds' flat. MacDonald, who had begun with an honorarium of just £25, was now provided with a salary sufficient to cover the employment of an assistant, Jim Middleton. No less significant, as a sign of cohesion as well as credibility, was the establishment in 1903 of a central fund for the payment of the parliamentary salaries as yet denied by the state.

In 1906 the LRC also made its first significant parliamentary breakthrough, returning the 29 MPs who then elected their own officers and constituted themselves the Labour Party. By the end of the decade, with the miners' affiliation, its parliamentary strength was over 40. This, while obviously dependent on organisation, was also a matter of strategy. Certainly, there was little about the British electoral system, except perhaps where there were dense occupational concentrations like the mining constituencies, that seemed conducive to translating Labour's growing support directly into seats. Confronted with an election almost on its foundation in 1900, the LRC gave little sign that it had sufficient independent support to displace the Liberals. Only two of its 15 candidates were elected, one being Hardie, and both depended on the tacit support of a Liberal running partner.[1] There was scant evidence here of the emergence of a significant Labour presence, at least for the foreseeable future. The only consolation, paradoxically, was that the Liberals by their own standards fared no better.

MacDonald's personal experience provided a striking example both of Labour's dilemmas and of its opportunities. In 1899 he had shifted his candidacy to Leicester, which like Southampton was a two-member constituency. The city had a long radical tradition and a thriving labour and socialist movement based in the footwear trades. The ILP tradition was particularly strong and provided a natural inducement to MacDonald to try his hand. At the same time, Leicester had for decades been politically dominated by the Liberals and there seemed to be no easy openings for a Labour candidate. Fighting in the difficult circumstances of the 1900 'Khaki' election, MacDonald came bottom of the poll, with less than half of the vote of any of his rivals, whether Liberal or Conservative. Despite the greater resources he had at his disposal,

James Keir Hardie (1856–1915) was the first independent Labour Member of Parliament, winning West Ham (South) by a majority of 1,232 in 1892. A lifelong trades unionist, he was known as 'the Member for the Unemployed'. In 1906 became first chairman of the 28-strong Parliamentary Labour Party. The best-known and most popular Labour figure of his day, as war approached in 1914 he attempted to organise the Socialist International to declare a general strike in all countries should war break out, but the failure of these plans, and the decision of the majority of the Labour Party to back the war when it came, deeply disillusioned him and he died a year later.

this represented no tangible advance on the performance of his ILP predecessor five years earlier. What MacDonald did once more achieve, however, was a sufficient incursion into the Liberal vote to let one of the Tories in. Thus he brought about the Liberals' first parliamentary setback in the constituency in 40 years. Of the four other constituencies in which Labour and Liberal candidates ran in opposition to each other, one was Hardie's Merthyr, while two of the others also saw Conservatives slip in on a split vote. As, after 1900, the LRC established the capacity to run a far greater number of candidates across the country, it was clear that its capacity to damage the Liberals would represent a formidable bargaining counter.

The issue needed handling carefully, not to say conspiratorially. On the one hand, the movement for Labour representation owed a good deal to political activists who were often as hostile to the Liberals as to the Tories. On the other hand, the whole issue of Labour representation had arisen in part because of the unwillingness of local Liberal caucuses to make constituencies available to Labour or socialist candidates. At a national level, for both MacDonald and his Liberal counterparts, the arguments for a national arrangement between the two parties were compelling. At the same time, such a tradeoff could only be made effective through the co-operation of constituency associations which in practice enjoyed considerable local autonomy. In Labour's case, there was also the ever-present threat of independent socialist candidates. There was also the possibility that a formal pact with Labour might alienate sections of the Liberal electorate, while Labour conversely might jeopardise its possible appeal to working-class Conservatives.

If a winner-takes-all system put a high premium on achieving some sort of agreement, the anomaly of the two-member constituency provided scope for horsetrading. In discussions of electoral reform, it is perhaps too seldom recalled how the one major realignment of the British party system in the 20th century was facilitated by this modest variation on the multi-member constituency. While lacking any element of proportionality, these two-member seats offered scope for both national and local bargaining without depriving local parties of the chance of getting their own candidate into Parliament. To a lesser extent the same was also true of the multi-constituency boroughs, in which again Labour had some of its best prospects of success. It was primarily on these lines that, over the two-and-a-half years following the 1900 election, MacDonald sought to prepare the ground for an electoral deal.

Through delicate interventions at the constituency level and the exercising of pressure on the Liberal whips he achieved in this form of the MacDonald-Gladstone pact of September 1903. Essentially, this was a gentleman's agreement with the Liberal whip, Herbert Gladstone, by which Gladstone agreed to use his influence to allow Labour a free run in some 30 seats, while Labour would demonstrate its 'friendliness' to the Liberals elsewhere. In reaching this agreement, MacDonald was supported throughout by Hardie, for the instinct for negotiation was not his alone. Nevertheless, the arrangement was not made public; and when necessary, as for example when a Labour candidate was threatened in Gladstone's own constituency, it was actively dissimulated or denied. Even so, only the credulous could have been unaware of the sorts of consideration that were coming into play in candidate selections. Of the 29 MPs Labour returned to Parliament in 1906, only four had done so against Liberal opposition. The Liberals for their part enjoyed a parliamentary landslide – one of only four such victories for the left across the entire 20th century.

The main issue in the election was that of free trade or protection, and here MacDonald like other Labour candidates came down firmly in favour of the former. Vindicated in his strategy, he made no secret of his vision of *a united democratic party appealing to the people on behalf of a simple, comprehensive belief in social reconstruction.* Whether or not this party called itself Liberal, he went on, *it will be as far ahead of Liberalism as Liberalism itself was of its progressive predecessor Whiggism.*[2] Whether this meant the supersession of the Liberal Party or its transformation was at this time still ambiguous.

Naturally, one beneficiary of the arrangement was MacDonald himself. The situation in Leicester was an awkward one, but with Gladstone's assistance he successfully manoeuvred his most serious Liberal rival into a Sheffield constituency, with the assurance there of Labour support. MacDonald thus entered Parliament with a Liberal running partner on what in many respects was a 'progressive' ticket. Though that was also true of several of his new parliamentary colleagues, MacDonald cut a distinctive figure in the new Parliamentary Labour Party (PLP). The great majority of his colleagues were trade unionists sponsored by their unions, although of course several were also members of the ILP. As their first officers, they elected Hardie as Chairman, Arthur Henderson as Chief Whip and MacDonald himself as Secretary. It was indicative of MacDonald's habitual jealousy of his most plausible rivals that on a finely balanced contest between Hardie as the leading socialist and the trade unionist David Shackleton he initially abstained.

Reflecting strong labour traditions of collective responsibility, the role of chairman was in any case very different from the later conception of party 'leader'. Hardie did not even aspire to such a role; nor did Labour's parliamentary situation at first demand such an innovation. Given the size of the Liberal majority, the PLP had very limited leverage over the government. Given its dependence on Liberal electoral support, it perhaps had little to desire to exercise any. The one issue on which it felt impelled to adopt a more distinctive stance was unemployment. On this MacDonald himself played an important role in moving Labour's so-called 'right to work bill' of 1907, and it was on this that he first won his parliamentary spurs. Nevertheless as a result of both its ethos and its parliamentary situation, the PLP in its first few years functioned very much as a parliamentary pressure group.

What transformed the situation were the elections of 1910. The issue on this occasion was that of the 'Peers against the People', on which again the Labour Party had no especially distinctive position. Nor did the year's two general elections see any significant advance in Labour's parliamentary representation. Instead, it was the recovery of the Conservative vote that deprived the Liberals of an independent majority and gave both Labour and the Irish Nationalists an

Philip Snowden (1864–1937) was one of the 29 independent Labour MPs elected in 1906, serving as MP for Blackburn until 1918. He opposed the First World War, lost his seat in 1918, and returned as MP for Colne Valley in 1922. He was Chancellor of the Exchequer in the first two Labour governments and Lord Privy Seal in MacDonald's National Government 1931–2. He believed in balanced budgets, a return to the Gold Standard and free trade. It was his proposal to cut unemployment benefit that split the Labour Party and led to the National Government.

influence they both coveted and partly dreaded. For Labour especially, the situation was in some ways an unenviable one. On the one hand, it felt constrained to maintain the government in office, not least because of the possible electoral consequences of failing to do so. On the other hand, it now came under unprecedented pressure from its own activists for a far more robust and independent political stance. Challenged on the one hand by the suffragettes, and on the other by striking miners, dockers and railway workers, the PLP's championship of the underdog seemed timorous in the extreme. Hardie and even Philip Snowden expressed the same concerns even from within the parliamentary party.

Much of the discontent focused on MacDonald. At the beginning of 1911, MacDonald was elected the PLP's chairman on the understanding that he vacate his post as party secretary in favour of Henderson. Hitherto the assumption had been that the position would be held for two years. MacDonald, however, seems to have accepted it on the understanding that he hold it indefinitely, like the conventional party leader that he clearly intended to become. More than any of his colleagues, MacDonald fitted the bill and he was sounded out more than once about joining Asquith's Cabinet. The reasons he gave for not accepting included his reluctance to support the government *through thick and thin* and the damage that he might cause the Labour Party if he did so.[3] There is no reason to doubt these motives. Nevertheless, there are two striking features of his career that might also be relevant. The first is that he never at Westminster demonstrated any particular administrative capacity or desire so to prove himself. The second, perhaps related to this, was that he had a profound sense of insecurity that made him warier of strong political personalities than of weak ones. In the 1920s this was certainly to be cited as one of the reasons why he preferred to keep his distance from Lloyd George. Occupying a junior position in a heavyweight Liberal cabinet might well have been less attractive to him than cutting a figure as Labour's acknowledged parliamentary star.

In any case, as far as the PLP's critics were concerned, supporting the government through thick and thin was precisely what MacDonald was doing. In industrial disputes, he functioned as a sort of intermediary for the government for whom dialogue and the reaching of agreement was the highest priority. In relation to the suffrage issue, he was hostile to the suffragettes, whom he felt invited martyrdom, and declined to use Labour's influence to force the government's hand.

Another of his ILP colleagues, J Bruce Glasier, observed that MacDonald lacked the 'instinct of agitation' and it is clear that he was deeply out of sympathy with the militant temper of the times.[4] Already he was propounding a characteristic version of ethical socialism as the alternative to any direct action to redress material injustices. *The appeal to class interest is an appeal to the existing order, whether the class addressed is the rich or the poor*, he wrote in 1911. *The motive force of Socialism is therefore not the struggle, but the condemnation of the struggle by the creative imaginative intelligence and by the moral sense.*[5] When in 1931 his second Labour government fell over the TUC's refusal to accept cuts in unemployment benefit, time and again it was the loss of *idealism and vision* in favour of *materialist arguments based on poverty* that he described as a betrayal of socialism.[6]

The appeal to class interest is an appeal to the existing order, whether the class addressed is the rich or the poor. The motive force of Socialism is therefore not the struggle, but the condemnation of the struggle by the creative imaginative intelligence and by the moral sense.

MACDONALD

Opinion remains divided as to how far Labour's displacement of the Liberals was already in 1914 a foregone conclusion. Increasingly, however, it is understood that neither the Liberal nor Labour parties had a fixed and immutable character at the time that war broke out and that the relations between them depended on intricate alignments and realignments, both at national and at local level. The onset of war immediately closed down some possible avenues. MacDonald was never again to be invited to join a Liberal government; and reflecting on the issue retrospectively, he would single out the foreign policy of Sir Edward Grey as an obstacle to his having done so.[7] At the same time, however, the opposition which Grey's policy provoked in both the Liberal and Labour parties was to open up the possibility of a rather different realignment. In a way impossible to have forecast before the war, MacDonald was to develop the most intimate cross-party relations while at the same establishing a new-found credibility with the left. It was a potent combination and one of its results was to be a MacDonald premiership.

Chapter 4: A Socialist at War: 1914–23

A curious feature of MacDonald's career is its demonstration of the law of unintended consequences. In 1931, its unwitting climax, by seemingly splitting the Labour Party he helped it coalesce around a clearer programme and identity in rejecting him than he could ever have provided as its leader. In 1914, the other decisive moment of his career, he took a principled stand on the war which appeared to mean the abandonment of his personal ambitions, only for him to realise them in less than a decade. It is fit material for a sermon. Holding onto office in 1931, he cast a blight on his political reputation from which it has never recovered. Relinquishing it in 1914, he showed a resolution in the face of adversity that proved central to his mystique as Labour's 'man of tomorrow'. But between these competing myths, as usual, the thread of Mac-Donald's career was more serpentine and unpredictable than it at first appears.

In the making of the first MacDonald myth, the war played a crucial role. A remarkable literary document of MacDonald's emerging cult is Molly Hamilton's *Man of Tomorrow*, published in an ILP edition on the eve of the first Labour government. The book's longest chapter is called 'The black years' and recounts the 'savage loathing' to which MacDonald was subjected during the war, whipped up by a jingo press. One of the metaphors Hamilton uses is that of MacDonald's stoning. The same metaphor was also used in this connection by Helen Swanwick in a commemorative history of wartime peace activities. These, of course, are just the sorts of accounts from which memories are made. Even Marquand's more measured treatment describes a campaign of 'extraordinary savagery' and cites a private informant: 'men still remember how he stood his ground at ILP meetings while being stoned by the mob.' The historian Kenneth Morgan, in a generally balanced overview, offers the opinion that 'no socialist leader has faced more intense persecution than MacDonald did in these wartime years'. If not a Christ-like figure, he became, as Hamilton suggested, a redemptive figure cast in Hardie's mould. He 'began sowing the seed ... and was stoned for it'.[1]

One need not underestimate the ugly mood of the times to regard these accounts as rather dramatic. In speaking out against the government's foreign policy, MacDonald showed considerable political courage. Because of his prominence, there is also no doubt that he attracted many of the most virulent press attacks. Nevertheless, his reservations about the war did not entirely overcome a native sense of caution and political strategy. It was characteristic, for example that the main vehicle for his peace activities should not have been the socialist anti-war campaigning of the ILP but the Union of Democratic Control (UDC). Initiated on the outbreak of war, the UDC was primarily a movement of advanced Liberals such as C P Trevelyan, E D Morel and Arthur Ponsonby. MacDonald was involved from the start, and as its sole prominent Labour figure his name was given first on the organisation's communications. As the UDC's name suggests, these aimed not only to set out markers for a negotiated peace but campaigned for parliamentary control over foreign affairs and an end to the secret diplomacy that was seen as one of the chief causes of the war. Issues such as the immediate cessation of the war were thus avoided. So too, until the spring of 1915, were public meetings. As the UDC's first draft circular put it, it was 'not advisable to hold indignation meetings or to take any public action until the country is absolutely secure from danger'.[2]

With Morel, MacDonald was initially the most outspoken of the UDC's leaders. Barely a week after the war's outbreak he used the pages of the ILP's *Labour Leader* to present a compelling indictment of British foreign policy. As he wrote to Morel a few days later:

In view of the daily statements that are appearing in the press defending the war we must not carry out too absolutely even at this moment our decision not to publish criticisms on the events of the last eight years.[3]

Such was the uproar caused by his articles that the essential moderation of his position was overlooked. Focusing as the UDC did on the diplomacy that had *preceded* the war and which MacDonald felt ought to *follow* it, he was initially a good deal more circumspect about the war itself. When in September 1914 he was invited to play his part in recruiting for the front, the terms in which he declined to do so were so elliptical as to cause bewilderment:

Victory ... must be ours. England is not played out. Her mission must be accomplished... . History will in due time apportion the praise and the blame, but the young men of the country must, for the moment, settle the immediate issue of victory... . To such men it is enough to say 'England has need of you', to say it in the right way.

Snowden, representing a more combative anti-war strain within the ILP, described this in his memoirs as an example of MacDonald's 'facility in dancing round the mulberry bush'.[4] Even Morel, who commended MacDonald's great personal courage, admitted wondering what his 'real game' was. 'He has a hundred little subtleties which keep me in a constant state of vigilance all the time ...'[5] In a sympathetic biography like Elton's, the point is effectively made that MacDonald combined an instinctive abhorrence of war with a sensitivity to what he saw as national interests now that the war had actually begun.

People do believe we are selling our country & that we are tainted as with leprosy. I came across it twice today in the golf club.

MACDONALD

The experience of ostracism also needs putting in perspective. MacDonald did receive hostile letters; London hostesses struck him off their lists; he had to take refuge, as Marquand puts it, at 'glittering' country-house weekends at Lady Ottoline Morrell's. If this was ostracism, it tells us a good deal about the sorts of circles in which MacDonald felt he belonged. *The opposition to us is tremendous*, he wrote to Trevelyan, with an unintended note of bathos.

So soon as one goes outside one's own immediate personal circle one meets it in the most cruelly oppressive way. People do believe we are selling our country & that we are tainted as with leprosy. I came across it twice today in the golf club. It is impossible to imagine until it is experienced.[6]

As we have seen, when subsequently he was struck off the club's membership it is said to have hit him harder than any other rebuff he experienced in the entire war.[7]

It was not even true that MacDonald had no support beyond his own immediate circle. Even overlooking the middle-class radical networks of the UDC, the treatment he received within the labour movement was far from universally hostile. Though he was in a minority over the war, Henderson, his successor, urged him to reconsider his resignation as Labour's parliamentary chairman. Remaining on the party executive as treasurer, he thus enjoyed that toleration of minority rights which had sometimes frustrated him before the war. Attending the 1915 TUC as Labour's fraternal delegate, he was greeted with prolonged cheering. The same thing happened at the Labour Party conference the following year; though typically some admitted confusion as to whether he was for the war or against it, applause 'burst forth from every part of the hall'.[8] As the war progressed, or failed to progress, the need for such equivocation passed. Hardie's death in 1915 meant that MacDonald was to enjoy the years of vindication without a rival, unless it were Snowden. But Snowden lacked his links with both the Clydesiders on the one hand and the UDC Liberals that were coming over to Labour on the other.

I have been through this before, and 1906 came as part recompense: thus MacDonald had defied his critics on the outbreak of war.[9] This time the recompense took longer but was much fuller when

A cousin of the late Queen Elizabeth the Queen Mother, Lady Ottoline Morrell (1873–1938) was a hostess, socialite and patroness of numerous artists and writers, including those known as the 'Bloomsbury Group', and D H Lawrence and Augustus John. During the First World War she and her husband, the Liberal politician Philip Morrell were noted pacifists, offering refuge at their home at Garsington to conscientious objectors such as the artist Duncan Grant. It was while on sick leave from the Western Front at Garsington that Siegfried Sassoon was persuaded to go absent without leave as a protest against the war.

it came. Rejected by his Leicester constituents in the post-war 'Khaki' election, MacDonald suffered a further setback on contesting the East Woolwich by-election of March 1921. Thanks to the renewed attentions of Horatio Bottomley, proprietor of *John Bull*, this was a squalid campaign and

MacDonald's supposed treachery was again to the fore. The immediate result was another defeat, albeit a narrow one, in solid Labour territory. Once again, however, MacDonald's reputation for resilience and dignity in the face of adversity was reinforced. Standing for the ILP's National Administrative Council later the same year, he easily topped the poll.

It was on this basis that at the end of 1922 MacDonald returned to the leadership of the Labour Party. Despite the continuing split within the Liberal Party, the election marked the return from coalition politics to more familiar forms of party competition. What was not familiar was Labour's new standing as a national party. Even discounting the Liberals' deep divisions, Labour almost matched them in the number of candidates and leapt ahead in both share of the vote and number of MPs. One of the successful candidates was MacDonald, who had been returned for the ILP stronghold of Aberavon.

In these circumstances, the election of the PLP's chairman took on a new significance: potentially as that of Labour's Prime Minister in waiting. The incumbent, J R Clynes, was well-regarded but uninspiring, the personification of trade union loyalism. MacDonald in the past four years had been contemptuous of the parliamentary performance of such

Horatio Bottomley (1860–1933) was a financier, journalist, politician and swindler who was one of the most colourful and disreputable characters of the late 19th and early 20th centuries. A bankruptcy in 1912 forced him to give up his parliamentary seat, but his 'patriotic' work during the First World War, publicised in his magazine *John Bull* (founded 1906) saw him returned as an Independent MP for Hackney in 1919. In 1921, after the failure of his 'John Bull Victory Bond Club' (a forerunner of Premium Bonds), he was gaoled for seven years for fraud and was expelled from Parliament.

figures. He had also kept himself in the movement's eye through the use of his journalistic skills, notably through the Glasgow *Forward*. It is to the Clydesiders, who were to be rapidly undeceived, that MacDonald's election as party leader is usually attributed. However, MacDonald could also count on a sizeable contingent of ex-Liberals, several of them, like Trevelyan, Ponsonby and Morel, having gravitated to Labour through the UDC. Even this might not have been enough to overcome Labour's union MPs, still in a majority, were it not that some 22 of them failed to attend the decisive meeting. Perhaps they failed to appreciate the factional significance it had now taken on. Perhaps their absence merely confirmed the criticisms made of their neglect of parliamentary duties. In any event, MacDonald was elected by just five votes, by 61 to Clynes's 56. There can never have been a British Prime Minister who was to go so far on minority votes.

1935
"I got the Job-
help me to
keep it"
FITZGERALD
OTE FOR THE
ATIONAL GOVERNMENT

Part Two

THE LEADERSHIP

Given Labour's ambitions as a party of social reform, it is not surprising that successive Labour premiers have been judged by their effectiveness in carrying through such a programme. Based on the achievements of his first three years in office, verdicts on Attlee have tended to be favourable. Registering the failure to carry through his early promise of modernisation, those on Wilson have been cautious and often hostile. Whether Blair leaves the memory of a further breach of promise or its fulfilment may be left to others to decide. In any case, and notwithstanding the complications of his foreign policy, it is on New Labour's record in transforming British society that the government is likely to be judged.

Ramsay MacDonald presents a rather different case. Perhaps the closest comparison is with James Callaghan, Labour's premier of 1976–9, whose main achievement in office was in remaining there at all. In both cases, the political context was that of a minority government in which Labour's survival in office depended upon the other non-Conservative parties. In both cases, the economic context was that of an international crisis in which their governments struggled simply to keep afloat. By the time they relinquished office, in 1935 and 1979 respectively, both could feel that economically they had seen the country through the immediate crisis. Expectations of purposeful programmatic government nevertheless seemed inconsistent both with parliamentary arithmetic and the perceived financial realities of the time.

Behind such essentially contingent factors, there is also a striking symmetry between the two periods of government. If on the one hand Callaghan's expediencies marked the exhaustion of the reforming dynamic of the Attlee years, MacDonald's Labour governments represented the attainment of office before the party really knew what to do with it. For each of the leaders, the result was a sort of nemesis. However, where Callaghan fell with his party in the open contest of a general election, MacDonald abandoned his to form a new administration with his erstwhile political adversaries. Here the only real parallel is with his Liberal rival, Lloyd George, who in 1918 achieved a similar parliamentary landslide but also at the head of a largely Conservative administration. It is not a comparison that flatters MacDonald. For whereas Lloyd George remained very much in control of his government, making deft and sometimes unscrupulous use of his prime-ministerial prerogatives, MacDonald was little more than the creature of his own parliamentary majority. Critics alleged that he was merely a cipher, and this was only underlined by the seamless succession of the Conservative Baldwin a few months before the 1935 election. Rambling, sometimes incoherent, MacDonald even then remained in the Cabinet as a minister without portfolio, leaving the final verdict to his Seaham constituents. They rejected him by a majority of more than two to one.

It is little wonder that such a career has become more than usually encrusted with myth. One MacDonald myth was that his actions of the summer of 1931 represented a cynical and calculated betrayal of his own party. Another was that they reflected a lonely sense of duty and commitment to the national interest, accepted almost in spite of himself. Neither of these myths is any longer tenable. Whether it demonstrates the integrity of his decision to form the National Government, or his limitations as a Labour leader in the years that preceded it, there is now general agreement that MacDonald's career both before and after the crisis was marked by a far greater degree of consistency than most contemporaries suspected. A third MacDonald myth has therefore to be guarded against: that of reconstructing his political career as if the denouement of 1931 was what it always had to lead to.

Few at least predicted such an outcome when MacDonald formed the first Labour government in January 1924. Well-known tales of countesses in terror of having their throats cut or the well-born heading for the coast with their valuables may no doubt be regarded as apocryphal.[1] Extreme as was the language of the patriotic right, the body of opinion it represented did not determine the responses of either of the established parties. Labour through Sidney Webb had the previous year proclaimed the inevitability of gradualness. Baldwin and Asquith, the Tory and Liberal leaders, now sought in the same spirit to accommodate its advance while as yet retaining a veto against any wilder tendencies to innovation. Had any real concerns over the constitution existed, the older parties would certainly have found the will to keep Labour out of office.

While all of this is clear in retrospect, contemporaries' sense of a moment of destiny should not entirely be submerged. Churchill, in transit from the Liberals to the Tories, described the government's formation as 'a serious national misfortune such as has usually befallen great States only on the morrow of defeat in war'. The communists, whose alleged influence partly underlay such lurid predictions, hailed it as a 'triumph' and pledged to secure from it a 'lasting victory for the cause of the workers'. Labour's own victory rally at the Albert

Hall was held in an atmosphere bordering on euphoria. Careful observers noted that the *Marseillaise* and *Red Flag* were interspersed with hymns. MacDonald apologised to the King for such residues of extremism, and the following year announced a competition to find the *Red Flag*'s replacement.[2] The sense of expectation, whatever its source of inspiration, was nevertheless immense.

We have built our finer habitations away on the horizon. We are a party of ideals. We are a party that away in the dreamland of imagination dwells in a social organisation fairer and more perfect than any organisation that mankind has ever known.

MACDONALD

MacDonald's mission in taking office was to dampen down both forebodings and the sense of anticipation and demonstrate Labour's fitness for office on the same terms as its opponents. Taking the platform at the Albert Hall, he dug deeply into the mystique of the pioneers and *the shield of love and the spear of justice* that Keir Hardie himself had wielded. Nevertheless, he was at pains to dispel any immediate expectation of a New Jerusalem.

We have built our finer habitations away on the horizon. We are a party of ideals. We are a party that away in the dreamland of imagination dwells in a social organisation fairer and more perfect than any organisation that mankind has ever known. (Cheers.) *That is true but we are not to jump there. We are going to walk there... . 'One step enough for me.'* (Laughter.)[3]

MacDonald could thus hardly be criticised for failing to take too many steps at once. The question was rather whether he knew what the first step was; and whether, as he put it at the Albert Hall, his first step would lead to another. After first discussing the prospects of office with his colleagues, MacDonald had noted privately: *Unanimous that moderation & honesty were our safety.*[4] It is on its moderation and honesty almost alone that Labour's new claims to office could be assessed.

Moderation was first of all demonstrated by the government's composition. The circumstances were in many ways distinctive. More so then than now, Labour represented a veritable hotchpotch of different tendencies, factions and organisational interests, notably including the trade unions. Cabinet-making, even at its most autocratic, was bound to register this. However, the crucial point in 1924 was that the Labour Party itself, in its developed form, was barely five years old. Ideologically, it was pluralistic. No working programme existed to provide a clear indication of priorities. Unions with longer histories than the party itself preserved a strong sense of prerogative, both individually and collectively. The diversity of career paths, whether within or beyond the labour movement, meant that measurements of service and seniority were more than usually fluid. Above all, the rules and conventions by which these different interests were to be reconciled were still in the process of being worked out. Though MacDonald had a multitude of considerations to attend to, he also had an unusual degree of latitude in attending to them.

He was in no doubt as to the course he should follow. Both his innate constitutionalism and the desire to shape a government according to his own predilections commended the precedent of Prime Ministerial control of Cabinet appointments. This was a period of considerable flux, not just within the Labour Party but within the party system as a whole. Though in due course cohesion was to be re-established around the new Labour-Tory axis, the transitional period of multi-party politics and minority government accentuated the opportunities for leadership initiative. 'Lloyd George lost his head, Mac is going the same way – even Baldwin plunged into a general election without consulting his friends',

Beatrice Webb observed of the new age of prime ministerial 'autocracy'.[5] In personally shaping his Cabinet in the wake of the election, MacDonald was merely setting the precedent that he would follow again in 1931.

His assumption of authority was the more emphatic in view of the unusual opportunities that existed for consultation. The outcome of the election in December 1923 had been that the Conservatives remained the largest party but lacked a mandate on the issue of protection on which they had gone to the country. There therefore followed an interlude of several weeks while the impending prospect of a minority Labour government was delayed until after the Christmas recess and the chance of a parliamentary vote of confidence. In a characteristic demonstration of his style of leadership, MacDonald in this crucial period decided to remove himself to Lossiemouth. The sole adviser he invited to join him was the recent Labour convert General C B Thomson, with whom MacDonald already had what he was to describe as a David and Jonathan relationship. Among MacDonald's closest colleagues there was broad acceptance that his should be the final voice in determining the Cabinet. Nevertheless, in removing himself from any possibility of meaningful collective deliberation, it is understandable that he should have provoked the resentment of senior colleagues like Snowden and Henderson.

Of course, there was much common ground on which all could have agreed. Labour's union MPs, for example, were visible but under-represented, with seven of the 20 Cabinet seats. This served to recognise their legitimate claims without too greatly taxing MacDonald's low estimation of their administrative capacities. Recent Liberal converts like Noel Buxton and Trevelyan were somewhat better represented. Principally this showed MacDonald's strategic sense both of their political qualities and of the significance for Labour's advance of the radical constituency which they represented. There was also obvious sense in the preferment of the Fabian Sidney Webb, while MacDonald also found a place for another of the original Fabian essayists, Sydney Olivier. Snowden's installation at the Treasury, as Labour's recognised financial expert, was generally regarded as a foregone conclusion. His relentless pursuit of economy in both the first and second Labour governments was to prove a decisive constraint on their capacity for innovation.

Others decisions were more indicative of MacDonald's personal priorities. One was the initial exclusion from his cabinet list of Arthur Henderson. Henderson, with Webb, was the major architect of the post-war national Labour Party. He was also the only leading figure who combined experience of cabinet government, in the wartime coalition, and an unbroken record of service to the labour movement. A trade unionist, former Liberal, Methodist lay preacher and personification of Labour's collective sense of loyalty, Henderson had had particularly fraught relations with MacDonald before the war. Nevertheless, when he succeeded him as parliamentary chairman in 1914 he behaved towards him with conspicuous fairness and sought to ensure that the route back to a leading position remained open to him. MacDonald's rationalisation of his proposed exclusion from the Cabinet in 1924 hinged on Henderson's importance to Labour's organisation in the country. Nevertheless, given his avowed concern regarding Labour's inexperience in government, the inference was naturally made of his wariness of a rival who more than matched his own credentials and had a closer rapport with the movement in the country. Though the episode was resolved with Henderson's appointment as Home Secretary, the memory of it was to continue to rankle.

The exclusion of the left may seem more predictable. It should not however be forgotten that it was through the left's support that MacDonald had secured the party leadership barely a year earlier. Most widely noticed was the omission of the militant and indiscreet Londoner, George Lansbury. More revealing, however, was the exclusion from any part of the government of MacDonald's former close associate E D Morel. Again Morel was a strong character whom MacDonald, as usual in such cases, found 'difficult'. His knowledge of foreign affairs was nevertheless unsurpassed and Trevelyan warned correctly that he would provide a powerful moral alternative if left outside the government.[6] The only left-wingers included were the veteran ILPer Fred Jowett and the new health minister John Wheatley, whom MacDonald reluctantly accepted *to keep the Clyde in*.[7]

MacDonald also appointed five ministers in the House of Lords. Nothing could have better demonstrated his conservative instincts and Snowden was right to observe that even the most timid of Labour's opponents took heart from such appointments There was at that time a convention that at least two secretaries of state be appointed from the Lords. With no existing Labour presence in the upper chamber, even this might usefully have been subject to some sort of challenge. MacDonald himself had proposed the abolition of the Lords as early as his Southampton candidacy in 1895 and thereafter had consistently expressed his preference for a single-chamber legislature. Nevertheless, his respect for the Lords' prerogatives now went beyond anything that was actually required of him. An appointment like that of the Conservative Viscount Chelmsford to the Admiralty can be explained by MacDonald's anxiety to assuage the establishment. So too can that of his friend and confidant General Thomson to the Air Ministry, on receipt of a peerage. In terms of power relations within the Cabinet, it is also clear that MacDonald could anticipate no credible challenge to his authority from ministers who lacked either a democratic mandate or, in certain cases, a Labour Party one. More generally in his advancement of former Liberals or Conservatives, MacDonald could feel a security in his own unassailable Labour credentials which could cut no ice with the likes of Henderson. Whatever the explanation, where MacDonald had five Cabinet ministers in the Lords, the Tory-based Lloyd George coalition had needed just three. This was like the forward march of Labour backwards.

MacDonald's most distinctive step was to act as his own Foreign Secretary. Though Gladstone had served as his own Chancellor, and Asquith had for a time taken on the War Office, the Tory Lord Salisbury alone had attempted this particular combination. With the growth of government since the turn of the century, only the most exceptional circumstances could have justified such a step. MacDonald's argument was that the very delicacy of the European situation required a Prime Minister's authority.[8] It was certainly the field in which his own expertise was greatest. It also offered scope for the grand gesture and mastery of rhetoric in which he excelled. Some, including Henderson, thought Arthur Henderson had better claims to the position. Radicals might have preferred Morel. MacDonald at first floated the ludicrous idea of appointing the bumptious J H Thomas, whom the whole of Europe would have laughed up its sleeve at. This invited precisely the suggestion that he would do better to take it on himself, which is credited with having come from his UDC colleague Arthur Ponsonby. Certainly Trevelyan, another UDC veteran, thought MacDonald's decision to act as Foreign Secretary the one thing that really mattered about the government. Hopes of a new era in international affairs were high. Only Snowden could have described the decision as a saving on the ministerial wages bill.

Europe at the start of 1924 was in sore need of some of Labour's idealism. Just four years after the Versailles treaty, Germany was in the grip of hyper-inflation. France had seized the opportunity to occupy the Ruhr. The USA had withdrawn to more immediate preoccupations. Soviet Russia still had something of a pariah status. MacDonald had been scathing about the performance in this field of his predecessors in Labour's parliamentary leadership. Now he saw the chance of constructive statesmanship in a field relatively unconstrained by the lack of a parliamentary majority. Nobody could have been more fluent in the radical rhetoric of the UDC. Few could have balanced this more delicately with the instinct of moderation.

In his *Policy for the Labour Party* published in 1920, MacDonald had singled out for criticism the reactionary character of the Foreign Office and repudiated *the plausible but pernicious theory of the 'continuity of Foreign Policy'.*[9] Nevertheless, even in opposition he had established with Baldwin a sort of foreign policy truce and privately acknowledged that the Conservative leader's views were *as near as matters, the same as mine.*[10] The main difference between the parties was over relations with Russia, and even these were entrusted by MacDonald to Ponsonby. That apart, the government's foreign and national security policy was almost bipartisan in character. Chelmsford and Thomson in the Lords provided not just symbolic assurance but the zealous advocacy of service interests. They were buttressed by Haldane, a former Liberal war minister, who had made it a condition of his serving as Lord Chancellor that he be released from day-to-day judicial sittings and allowed to chair the important Committee for Imperial Defence.[11] Commitments to a modified warship building programme (the 'five cruisers') and the development of air power disappointed radicals and the *Times* itself commended Labour's 'largeness of mind' in ignoring them.[12] Already, in looking askance at wartime campaigns against conscription, MacDonald had insisted that the only alternative to militarism was an international peace policy. Pending the achievement of such a policy, perhaps it was only logical that he should give no encouragement to similar acts of disengagement on the part of the state itself.

His commitment to multilateral negotiations, on the other hand, was genuine and even energetic. MacDonald's limitation as a politician was that his talents were essentially those of the performing artist. In the difficult international circumstances of the 1920s, on the other hand, this was precisely what the situation seemed to demand. Entering office in a period of high tension and diplomatic deadlock, MacDonald's informal approach to foreign affairs seemed like a manifesto in itself. The veteran Liberal journalist Henry Nevinson

James Henry Thomas (1874–1949) was one of Britain's best-known trade unionists, who by the 1920s combined the roles of Labour politician and general secretary of the National Union of Railwaymen. Politically and industrially a moderate, Thomas combined an undisguised relish for the trappings of office with the bluff vulgarity of a music-hall turn. As Lord Privy Seal in the second MacDonald government – characteristically, he described his office as 'more privy than seal' – he personified its incapacity to meet the challenge of mass unemployment and was shifted to the Dominions office. A staunch MacDonald loyalist, he followed his leader into the National Government and fell from office after leaking budget secrets in 1936.

even described him as transforming the 'whole atmosphere of European relations' by mere friendliness of demeanour.[13] In all MacDonald's governments, even when he ceased to function as his own Foreign Secretary, his most significant personal achievements were in the field of international relations.

With Ponsonby handling Russia, reparations and security, in that order, were at the top of his agenda. His impact on both belies the customary image of his dithering. The reparations imposed on Germany in 1919 had been denounced by Labour in opposition and seemed to many to be at the root of Europe's economic and security problems alike. Some have even argued that the high point of MacDonald's entire career was his successful convening of the London conference that achieved a settlement of the reparations question in August 1924. The basis of this settlement was the Dawes Plan published by a committee of experts in April 1924. Critics observed that by resolving the issue on the basis of the Versailles treaty, and thereby temporarily helping to stabilise it, the agreement was hardly consistent with Labour's previous opposition to the treaty. Questions were justifiably asked as to how different MacDonald's stance was from that which a Conservative government might have adopted. The answer, which was not always to apply to MacDonald, must have lain in the sense of urgency he brought to the issue. The election in the spring of Edouard Herriot's radical government in France also played an important part. Nevertheless, the role of MacDonald's new style of diplomacy, at once relaxed and energetic, received a good deal of the credit. That this might just as well have been the work of the Tory Lord Curzon on the one hand, or Jimmy Thomas on the other, would hardly have seemed worthy of consideration.[14]

With the way now cleared for security issues, MacDonald's other achievement was in helping engineer the abortive Geneva Protocol of October 1924. In providing for a system of arbitration back up by sanctions this was of a similarly ambiguous character. In September 1924, as the first British

The legacy of Versailles

Established in 1920 under a covenant of the post-war peace treaties, the League of Nations seemed the key to whatever prospects there existed of a lasting peace in Europe. For the first time in history the covenant pledged its signatories 'to promote international co-operation and to achieve international peace and security by the acceptance of obligations not to resort to war, by the prescription of open, just, and honourable relations between nations, by the firm establishment of the understandings of international law as the actual rule of conduct among Governments, and by the maintenance of justice and a scrupulous respect for all treaty obligations in the dealings of organised peoples with one another'. Despite these fine intentions, the 'treaty obligations' thus upheld included the punitive provisions of the Versailles Treaty of 1919 and the proposed exaction of 132 billion marks in reparations from Germany. This was a fatal contradiction and the League was arguably doomed from the start. The USA, which did not ratify the Versailles Treaty, was never a member. Nor at first were defeated Germany or revolutionary Russia, which with some justification described the League as a 'thieves' kitchen'. For MacDonald and the Labour Party, supporting the League but opposing punitive sanctions, a coherent foreign policy had somehow to reconcile these contradictions. For a period the the rescheduling of reparations payments under the Dawes plan of 1924 did seem to provide a basis for reconciliation. The French occupation of the Ruhr, intended to enforce payment, was ended. Committing itself to the peaceful resolution of its grievances, Germany entered the League in 1925 and a brief period of relative stability ensued. Nevertheless, renewed stresses arising from economic and political crisis after 1929 revealed that the League continued to lack both legitimacy and credibility. The fascist dictators of the 1930s treated it with open scorn, and within twenty years of the League's formation Europe was again at war. It took the more ambitious European projects of the post-1945 period, based this time on genuine Franco-German co-operation, to provide for a more enduring European peace, albeit initially circumscribed by the 'iron curtain' of the Cold War years.

Prime Minister to address the League of Nations, MacDonald had won over delegates with the impassioned case he made for international arbitration and disarmament. Geneva, where the League sat, was the perfect setting for his high-minded if often nebulous rhetoric. Literally he described arbitration as a system of watching out for clouds: *of warning when a cloud, just the size of a man's hand, appears above the horizon, and the taking of steps at once, not of a military kind but of a rational and judicial kind, to charm it out of existence. The test is, Are you willing to arbitrate? ... Are you afraid of the world? Are you afraid of the daylight, a lover of darkness and timorous lest the world should know what is in your mind?*[15] Read in cold print, knowing of all the disillusionments that were to follow, it is difficult to recapture the impression that his speeches appear to have made. Nevertheless, a seasoned observer described him as addressing the League, not as a diplomat might have done, but as a prophet.[16]

The test is, Are you willing to arbitrate? ... Are you afraid of the world? Are you afraid of the daylight, a lover of darkness and timorous lest the world should know what is in your mind?

MACDONALD

The negotiations which followed to give force to these sentiments fell to Lord Parmoor, one of the Cabinet's peers, and Arthur Henderson. There is some debate as to how keen MacDonald would have been to sign the protocol they negotiated had he still been in office. Already prefiguring the tensions of the 1930s, the provision made for sanctions, essentially on French insistence but with Henderson's support, must have seemed to him like the steps 'of a military kind' which he specifically disavowed. In broad terms he was to acclaim the protocol as *the substitution of a peace system for a war system.*[17] At the same sought to restore the emphasis by which he set such store on the creation of a new spirit in international affairs.

The new order of the Protocol will be its own sanction, he observed in opposition, staking his faith on the *new habits of honour* which the protocol would engender.

It brands crime as crime with the consent and signature of nations; it supplants a system of force by one of justice; it inculcates new habits of negotiation ... So soon as it has worked once or twice, it will be impossible for a nation to defy it ... not owing to the menace of force, but to habit and other psychological reasons ... The era of peace will have come at last.

MacDonald himself had prevaricated over signing the protocol, ostensibly because of the impending election, but also due to pressure from his service chiefs. With responsibility now falling to the incoming Conservative government, he was spared what might have been an uncomfortable dilemma. The Conservatives did not ratify it, and the promise of MacDonald's rhetoric remained to be tested.

Nevertheless, as a whole MacDonald was not ineffective as a Foreign Secretary. Where problems arose from his decision to take on two offices was not in relation to foreign affairs, but in his overall competence as Prime Minister. In extenuating his lapses of judgement, much has been made of the pressure under which he worked. Sympathetic contemporaries stressed the sheer workload that explained his unsureness of touch with the wider party. MacDonald himself began to adopt the tone of weary affliction that in his later years in office was to become his prime ministerial trademark. But the pressures he faced in 1924 were of his own making.

The Cabinet itself functioned poorly. Lord Haldane, who had other experience of other Cabinets, made a point of commending MacDonald's skilful chairmanship. Compared to Asquith, who tolerated the most meandering discussions, he must have seemed admirably businesslike, and his ministers 'trained ... by Trade Union discipline' to make their points succinctly.[18] What the Cabinet lacked was not dispatch but effective direction and co-ordination. If MacDonald was an autocrat, he was a weak and overburdened autocrat, and a 'mystery man' to his colleagues. As Beatrice Webb again put it: 'It is one-man-government, undiluted in so far as the PM's work is concerned; and one-man-government in each department until the department gets into a mess.'[19]

'It is one-man-government, undiluted in so far as the PM's work is concerned; and one-man-government in each department until the department gets into a mess.'

BEATRICE WEBB

Certainly, the government had little to show for its domestic record. The capital levy, its most distinctive economic proposal, was dropped. Trade union supporters were disappointed by its readiness to use emergency powers legislation against strikers. Above all, nothing of significance was done about unemployment, which had provide Labour with one of its main campaigning issues. MacDonald made an easy target for the opposition; his eyes were 'so fixed on the foreign horizon that he is stumbling over his own doormat'.[20] His response to such criticisms seemed more addressed to his own supporters:

Why should I not confess it? … Until you have been in office, until you have seen those files warning Cabinet Ministers of the dangers of legislation, or that sort of thing, you have not had the experience of trying to carry out what seems to be a simple thing, but which becomes a complex, an exceedingly difficult and laborious and almost heartbreaking thing when you are to be a member of a Cabinet in a responsible Government.[21]

Embedded in this confession of impotence was what proved to be a characteristic refrain: that government was a skilled and complicated business; that only those who exercised its responsibilities could make judgements as to what was feasible; and that they should therefore be left to make those judgements without constraint of binding programmes.

What limited achievements there were came from individual ministerial initiative. By common consent, the most significant domestic reform was the Wheatley Housing Act of August 1924. Housing, and the broken promise of homes for heroes, was another of the key political issues of the day, and workable ideas had already been developed should any minister want to make use of them. Nevertheless, it was Wheatley who took the plaudits both for his drive in initiating such a programme and his skill in shepherding it through parliament. Even Snowden was assuaged by the spread of costs over 60 years, and by the time of its repeal in 1933 the act had provided subsidies for some half a million local authority homes. For MacDonald, this represented both achievement and threat. The Liberal Charles Masterman described Wheatley as the parliament's one conspicuous success; Beatrice Webb noted his amazing *réclame* as the government's greatest parliamentarian.[22] Combining ability,

John Wheatley (1869–1930), the son of a Scottish miner, had joined the ILP in 1907 and was elected to the Lanarkshire County Council and the Glasgow Corporation. By 1920 he was the leading Labour figure in the city and in 1922 was one of the ten Labour candidates elected to Parliament for Glasgow. As Minister for Health in the 1924 Labour government, he rejected H G Wells' calls for birth control reforms due to his Catholic beliefs. A staunch left-winger, he opposed MacDonald's move to the right in 1929. He died of a stroke in 1930.

commitment and Clydeside credibility, it would have been unlike MacDonald had Wheatley not provoked a sense of pique and rivalry. In any event, the most successful minister in MacDonald's first government was to be found no place in his second.

While much can be explained by the lack of a parliamentary majority, MacDonald showed little sense of initiative even where no such constraint existed. For example, no attempt was made to remove the differential age qualifications introduced with women's suffrage in 1918. Here there could be no Treasury veto on radicalism, while the possibility of cross-party support was shown just four years later when the Conservatives themselves rectified the anomaly. MacDonald, however, denied time for a private members' bill on the issue, as if oblivious to the obvious political benefits of doing so as well as considerations of principle. 'It would have been a relatively simple matter ... to have adopted the bill and put it through its remaining stages', Cheryl Law has commented. 'The advantage to Labour's reputation would have been great, as would the gains at the ballot box.'[23] In domestic affairs at least, MacDonald-style progressivism represented little more than a dilution of Labour's traditional economic agendas, not a broadening out of them.

If safety lay in moderation, it was both appropriate and ironical that the government should have fallen over its perceived affinities with Communism. In August it concluded two draft treaties with Soviet Russia, including controversial provisions for a possible Soviet loan. The outcry this provoked was in part provoked by the intervention in the negotiations of a group of left-wing MPs led by Morel, who thereby enjoyed a brief moment of vindication. Matters were then compounded by the government's decision to drop charges of incitement to mutiny against the editor of a communist newspaper which had published a 'Don't shoot' appeal to British soldiers. It was this so-called Campbell case that the Cabinet decided to treat as an issue of confidence; and it lost the crucial Commons vote on 8 October. The election campaign that followed was further enlivened by the *Daily*

Mail's publication of the forged Zinoviev letter, which all too conveniently documented the seditious intent of the outgoing government's treaty partners.

If moderation proved no refuge, MacDonald's honesty was called into question too. Over the Campbell case itself, his unequivocal assurance that he had not been consulted over the proposed proceedings was privately described by the Director of Public Prosecutions as a 'bloody lie'. MacDonald characteristically admitted having gone *a little further than I ought to have gone* in making the statement. Snowden described how his colleagues wanted to hang their heads in shame.

Already MacDonald had suffered a similar erosion of credibility over the so-called 'McVitie's biscuits affair'. Shortly after taking office, he had imprudently accepted the private loan of a Daimler and £40,000 in McVitie's shares, *so that I may not require, whilst absorbed in public duties, to worry about income.* Still more imprudently, he then nominated his benefactor, a Scottish businessman called Alexander Grant, for a baronetcy. MacDonald himself had been used to denounce of the sale of honours as the worst manifestation of the plutocratic spirit in British politics. Claims that he had

Lloyd George while Prime Minister had effectively sold honours, through his agent Maundy Gregory, to raise funds for political campaigning, which lead to the passing of the Honours (Prevention of Abuses) Act 1925, criminalising such activity. It is allegations of breaking this law that have triggered a police investigation of the present government. Senior Labour figures are alleged to have rewarded businessmen who 'loaned' (thus avoiding disclosure regulations on gifts) the Labour Party money for campaigning with peerages, and also to have promised knighthoods etc, to those who sponsored the government's flagship trust schools.

not suspected the possible connection between the loan and peerage nomination were simply incredible. It was one of the less edifying precedents that he was to leave for his Labour successors.[24]

These hardly seemed ideal circumstances for an election. Nevertheless, it was not Labour that lost out by the polarisation of opinion, but the Liberals. Partly this was due to a fall in the number of Liberal candidates, and here the forms of multi-party competition had complex effects. Though the increase in Labour candidacies cut right into the Liberal vote, the withdrawal of Liberals served simultaneously to consolidate the forces of anti-socialism and hence reduce Labour's parliamentary representation. In other words, Labour picked up votes but lost out in seats. Paradoxically, it required the stronger Liberal showings of 1923 and 1929 to divide the anti-socialist vote and make possible Labour's experiments in minority government. Conversely, the contraction of Liberalism served to damage Labour's parliamentary strength while at the same time bolstering the two-party logic by which it was gradually supplanting the older party as the sole viable alternative to the Tories. Underlying its immediate electoral debacle, this was to be the message even in 1931. In 1924, as Labour lost almost a quarter of its MPs while increasing its popular vote by more than a million, the underlying pattern was even stronger.

Chapter 6: Rectitude of Thought, Consideration of Action: the Second Labour Government, 1929–31

By the time that Labour returned to office in 1929, MacDonald had consolidated his hold as Labour leader. Immediately following the 1924 election, there had been considerable discontent in Labour's ranks and many thought his leadership under threat. The 1925 elections for the parliamentary executive showed a sharp swing to the left with Lansbury heading the list. The same year's TUC proclaimed the sort of union-sponsored militancy that was anathema to the Labour leader. Even MacDonald's relations with his old base of the ILP came under irreparable strain. MacDonald himself clearly felt the pressure. In June he caused a minor upset by his over-reaction to a somewhat inconsequential communication from a local ILP branch. *Perhaps*, he burst out, *it would mind its own business and regard Socialism, not as the creed of a lot of blithering easie-oosie asses, who are prepared to pass any resolution without knowing its meaning, and on any subject without understanding it, but as something which requires rectitude of thought and considera- tion of action.*[1] The distance between the leader and his 'easie-oosie' rank and file appeared to be widening.

He was to emerge from such difficulties only the stronger for it. Through the successful marginalisation of the Com- munists, left-wingers like Lansbury were either put on the back foot or brought within the fold. With the 1926 General Strike, the alternative of direct action suffered a setback from which it did not recover during his lifetime. At the same time, neither the unions nor the ILP were able to maintain their predominance in the sponsorship of Labour's parliamentary candidates. Instead, through the medium of the constituency parties, there was consolidated a new class of largely middle-class parliamentary candidates, congenial to MacDonald and in many cases owing him a strong personal loyalty.

Lord Thomson was killed in the when the airship *R 101, en route* to India on her maiden voyage, crashed into a hill near Beauvais in France in the early hours of 5 October 1930 and burst into flames. Of the 54 people aboard, only six survived. The flight was supposed to inaugurate an Empire-spanning airship service, of which Thomson was a keen supporter, but the loss of the *R 101* spelled the end of British rigid airships, all that remains today of this prestige project being the giant airship sheds at Cardington in England.

When Labour had its next chance at the polls in May 1929 nearly two-thirds of its candidates were sponsored by the constituencies. For the first time these outnumbered union nominees even among Labour's 287 MPs. Though still some way off a majority, Labour was now the largest party; though the Conservatives, with 260 MPs, retained a slightly higher share of the popular vote. The Liberals, despite a last serious attempt to present themselves as a party of government, had just 59 MPs. MacDonald found himself back in Downing Street; and as the German observer Egon Wertheimer commented, he was more firmly in the saddle than ever.[2]

By most accounts he was more aloof from his colleagues as ever. Wertheimer again remarked on his 'deliberate isolation' from colleagues, his 'schoolmasterly' condescension, his hypersensitivity and vanity: 'He moves today in a personal vacuum that is almost painful to behold.'[3] The death of his close friend Thomson in an air crash in 1930 was to deprive him still further of his closest Labour confidant. This lack of any real collective leadership was to have dramatic consequences in 1931.

Even so, the coming of MacDonald's second Cabinet had been long anticipated and certain protocols for its formation were now accepted. Though MacDonald remained undisputed Cabinet-maker, he did now consult more formally with an inner group comprising Thomas, Henderson and Snowden. These, with the addition of Clynes, had come to be regarded as Labour's 'Big Five'. Along with Webb, they had already begun holding weekly lunches during the course of Mac-Donald's first government. Were it not for strong personal antagonisms and weak political leadership they might have provided an effective team.

Beyond them, there was considerable continuity between the Cabinets of 1924 and 1929. Eleven of MacDonald's colleagues from 1924 survived into his second Cabinet. Six of them, crucially including Snowden, returned to the same posts. The most important casualty was Wheatley, whom a tamed Lansbury succeeded as a less formidable concession to the left. Initially beyond the Cabinet, younger politicians were emerging like Clement Attlee, Hugh Dalton and Herbert Morrison, who was elevated to the Cabinet in March 1931. These were to provide the core of the Attlee government of 1945 and the experience of 1929–31 provided them with a cautionary tale from which they were to derive much benefit. The reckless Oswald Mosley, who seemed to some the most brilliant of them, resigned from the government in May 1930 and by the end of the year was passing through the New Party *en route* for fascism. Few were prepared to follow him, but the sense of malaise that Mosley expressed was widely shared.

Following another damaging clash of wills, formal responsibility for foreign policy now rested with Henderson. Once again, MacDonald originally proposed Thomas, who was devoted to him personally and merely lacked aptitude, experience and *gravitas*. Henderson, who had all three, demurred, and MacDonald again proposed combining the two positions. Perhaps, as in 1924, proposing Thomas had been meant to underline the preferability of even half of MacDonald. With obvious reluctance, MacDonald gave way to Henderson's refusal to serve in any other position, but as Prime Minister was persistently to encroach upon his territory and prerogatives.

Apart from their obvious personal rivalry, it was in foreign affairs that MacDonald knew best how to make his own mark. From the start, he assumed direct responsibility for Anglo-American relations, which had deteriorated badly on account of the two countries' naval rivalries. Encouraged by Herbert Hoover's recent installation as US president, MacDonald saw the opening for the sort of fireside diplomacy through which he might overcome the deadlock of entrenched positions. The trip he made to America in October 1929 was the first by a British Prime Minister in an official capacity and occasioned some ceremony. Welcomed in New York by a 19-gun salute and ticker-tape parade; staying on the President's ranch, addressing the Senate in what must have seemed Wilsonian tones: it all added up to a public relations triumph. In a century of British decline, this was the first such performance by a British premier. It was by no means to be the last.

MacDonald himself took the main responsibility for the negotiations that followed, presiding over the five-power London naval conference of January–April 1930. Rather like the unemployment problem, it seemed a lot more difficult to resolve these issues when you had to do it yourself. Seeking to establish an agreed naval balance of power, MacDonald and his interlocutors proved unable to circumvent the complexity of inter-state rivalries and apprehensions. Though Britain, Japan and the USA did manage to agree a formula, this key provision of the treaty did not therefore apply to the other signatories, France and Italy. This was a severe disappointment. Nevertheless, had these limited provisions paved the way for further disarmament, as MacDonald hoped, they would perhaps have been recognised as an important first step in the right direction. International affairs, however, were to take an altogether different course. It took the Japanese attack on Manchuria less than two years later to show that clouds lay on the horizon that no amount of charm would be sufficient to dispel.

It would be anachronistic simply to indict MacDonald for this, as was sometimes attempted in the backlash against appeasement. Nevertheless, even at this early stage dilemmas over collective security can be traced in the political as well as personal tensions that existed between MacDonald and Henderson. Briefly resurfacing at the time of the Geneva protocol, these tensions can be traced back to the contrasting positions they adopted towards the First World War. Where Henderson, very crudely, recognised the need to bolster arbitration by the threat of force, MacDonald's ideal was of diplomacy as an alternative to force. They clashed over the issue near the start of Henderson's tenure as Foreign Secretary, when he signalled British support for measures at the League of Nations aiming to buttress collective security by financial assistance to the victims of aggression. Alarmed by the press reaction in Britain, MacDonald sought to countermand his authority. Henderson responded with considerable firmness and the matter appears to have been dropped.

Almost throughout the period of the government, MacDonald continued to devote his best efforts to performances on the international stage. At Geneva he orated brilliantly. In London, he presided not only over the naval conference of January–April 1930 but over the imperial conference of October–November 1930 and the Indian Round Table conference of November 1930–January 1931. Add in his holidays in Lossiemouth, and that amounted to virtually half the year, and the same neglect of domestic affairs as in his first government. Some were unkind enough to suggest that the conflict of interests was not unwelcome to him. 'More than all', his parliamentary private secretary remembered acidly, 'a conference gave MacDonald the excuse for absence from the House of Commons ... [where] there was always the risk of being pestered by Ministers actually wanting something done.'[4] Certainly, there were things enough to pester him about.

The main one was unemployment. Although the unemployed figures appeared to have stabilised at a little over a million, unemployment had inevitably been one of the major issues in the 1929 election. Very largely this was due to Lloyd George's dramatic commitment to reduced unemployment to 'normal' levels through an ambitious public works programme. Labour in response had also promised a managed reduction in unemployment, only to be confronted with a crisis of a different order of magnitude from anything it could have anticipated. Just six months after it entered office, the Wall Street Crash dragged down Europe's economies in the wake

'More than all, a conference gave MacDonald the excuse for absence from the House of Commons ... [where] there was always the risk of being pestered by Ministers actually wanting something done.'

L MACNEILL WEIR

of the American crisis. Britain, which was not the worst affected, saw a virtual doubling of unemployment, to nearly 2.75 million, by the end of 1930. MacDonald described it as an economic blizzard, and the following year as a typhoon.[5] It was the Prime Minister against an act of God; or, if there could have existed a being still more forbidding and unbending, against his Chancellor Philip Snowden.

The issue of how to deal with unemployment has sometimes been seen as a battle between economic radicals and economic conservatives.[6] Snowden without a doubt was one of the latter; and as so often in Labour's history, the need for a counterweight to the Treasury view was imperative if perceived financial interests were not to predominate over all other social goals. At the same time, one of the lessons of Labour's experience in 1924 was of the need for a figure in government who could bring a broader perspective to bear on possible initiatives than was possible for any single department.

Goaded perhaps by Lloyd George, there was even talk in the election of an economic general staff. Indeed, MacDonald briefly imagined adopting such a style of leadership himself:

This time I must develop the work of the PM so as to co-ordinate the State policy of the various departments … I want to create a real advisory committee for the PM, a body that will work out schemes, watch developments, conduct investigations & generally, keep the machinery of Government running steadily. Our conception of the functions of Government means a new position for the PM & I must work at that. Unemployment will also require much attention from the PM.[7]

It was all too good to be true. MacDonald did entrust the faithful Thomas with oversight of the unemployment issue, supported by a talented team comprising Lansbury, Mosley and Thomas Johnston. Thomas, however, was clearly out of his depth. As early as the summer of 1929, MacDonald had confessed to having had *no idea before we came into office how precarious was the condition of the country*:

Everything that mortal man can do is being done to devise schemes and meet the problem … and yet there is practically nothing up to now to show for it.[8]

Initially supported by Lansbury and Johnston, Mosley in January 1930 presented more radical proposals for an expansionist programme depending on strong executive action by the government. On the Cabinet's failure to act upon these he resigned from the government four months later.

In theory this was when MacDonald stepped in. Thomas, now an obvious liability, was moved to Dominions. He was replaced by the South Wales miners' MP Vernon Hartshorn, a veteran of the first Labour Cabinet who was provided with a secretariat of civil servants headed by Sir John Anderson. Already in January, MacDonald had taken the initiative in establishing an economic advisory council, combining expert advisers like Keynes with representatives of the two sides of industry. Now he also took charge of a panel of ministers to develop unemployment policy, with Hartshorn as his deputy. The machinery, or some machinery, was there. The will to make use of it was not.

Was this because of MacDonald's preoccupation with other commitments? Or were these simply the pretext for his incapacity even to focus properly on the subject? The unemployment panel barely functioned. Hartshorn's complaint was that he could hardly even get to speak to MacDonald, let alone get him to discuss unemployment.[9] In August 1930 he drafted a long memorandum which MacDonald commended in fulsome terms. *You set out questions which we must consider and answer, if the next session is to bring us any credit*, he noted, but then he added a significant rider: *It is most unfortunate that some of us will be able to give practically no attention to the subject on this side of Christmas.*[10]

If public works presented one way of thinking about the problem, the introduction of tariffs was another. Pessimistic about public works, Hartshorn in his memorandum had hinted at the possibility of fiscal reforms. MacDonald at least was amenable to such ideas. To Snowden, however, they were anathema. Fortuitously, the issue of a tariff moratorium was due to come before the Cabinet just a fortnight after Hartshorn produced his memorandum. MacDonald, in a classic demonstration of his leadership, simply absented himself in Lossiemouth while Snowden carried the day. In October he wrote again to Hartshorn urging him to keep the whole question alive, but excusing himself from meeting him because of the imperial conference. Two months later it was the Indian Round Table: *My work just now is so pressing, and subdivision of labour is so necessary, that I am thinking of nothing but India.*[11] As Lloyd George acerbically put it in the debate on the King's Speech, MacDonald was simply 'too busy to do his job'.[12]

> My work just now is so pressing, and subdivision of labour is so necessary, that I am thinking of nothing but India.
>
> MACDONALD

There is something to be said for the view that the government's limitations were simply those of the received economic wisdom of the day. Labour's problem was that it had raised expectations of going beyond those limitations. From the original Fabians to the post-war revisionists and beyond, Labour reformists have always conceived of their social programmes being paid for out of the surplus of an expanding economy. The bankruptcy of the MacDonald years was that they had no faintest notion of how to generate such a surplus. Their approach to unemployment benefits was slightly less punitive and humiliating than the Conservatives', and they would have liked the difference to be wider. The scapegoating of MacDonald was to obscure the fact that they had no real idea of how to go about it.

One of the ironies of the MacDonald years was that a narrowly economic conception of socialism provided the basis for Labour's fragile party unity, and yet it was on its economic programme – or lack of one – that Labour was least of all able to deliver. The overall record of the government offered little enough in its place. A housing act, this time focused on slum clearance, was again among the exceptions. So were provisions for agricultural marketing boards and the reorganisation of London transport, signalling the sort of administrative rationalisation that was to become a hallmark of the National Government. There was also a Coal Mines Act which sought to balance commitments over working hours with the owners' desire for quotas. Beyond some token concessions to the Liberals, it did nothing about the industry's archaic structure. An education bill to raise the school leaving age did not even reach the statute book, though this would have had a favourable impact on levels of unemployment. Economy was one reason, for Snowden had refused to meet

'I remember, when I was a child, being taken to the celebrated Barnum's circus, which contained an exhibition of freaks and monstrosities, but the exhibit … which I most wished to see was the one described as "The Boneless Wonder". My parents judged that the spectacle would be too revolting and demoralising for my youthful eyes, and I have waited 50 years to see the boneless wonder sitting on the Treasury Bench.' (Winston Churchill, speaking of Ramsay MacDonald, in the House of Commons, 28 January 1931: *The Oxford Dictionary of Quotations* [Oxford University Press, Oxford: 1979] p 149.)

the costs of the reform in denominational schools. The consequent objections of the churches to the bill was the other. The Education Secretary, Charles Trevelyan, resigned in the spring of 1931, though by that time it hardly mattered.

The circumstances of the government's fall have been minutely scrutinised. Responding to opposition pressures for reductions in expenditure, in March 1931 it appointed an economy committee chaired by the retiring secretary of the Prudential, Sir George May. Nominated equally by each of the three parties, both the committee and its terms of reference marked a big step towards a cross-party approach. At the same time, it could be seen as Snowden's way of bringing pressure to bear on Cabinet colleagues reluctant to approve economies on the scale he thought necessary. The committee's report was published on 31 July, just after Parliament departed for the summer recess. Predicting a government deficit of £120 million, it proposed economies of £96 million included a 20 per cent cut in unemployment benefits.

'For himself he {MacDonald} would help us get these proposals through, though it meant his death warrant, but it would be of no use for him to join a Government. He would be a ridiculous figure unable to command support and bring odium on us as well as himself.'

NEVILLE CHAMBERLAIN

This was more than either the TUC or the majority of the Cabinet were prepared to support. By 23 August the Cabinet was deadlocked and MacDonald asked his colleagues to place their resignations in his hands. Recriminations were to follow as to how far he was already scheming to head a cross-party administration and, allegedly, had long intended to. Contemporary accounts suggest that as late as the evening of 23 August, when he met opposition leaders, he remained undecided as to his course of action. 'For himself he would help us get these proposals through, though it meant his death warrant', the Conservative Neville Chamberlain recorded in his diary, 'but it would be of no use for him to join a Government. He would be a ridiculous figure unable to command support and bring odium on us as well as himself.'[13] Perhaps this demonstrated the genuine reluctance to remain in office that MacDonald still had to overcome. Or perhaps it gave the signal that it was only by remaining as Prime Minister that his sense of duty could be properly aroused and acted upon. At the very least it seemed as if MacDonald was not prepared to provide any government with the benefit of his credibility while serving in some lesser capacity. The evidence is inconclusive and will no doubt remain so. What we do know is that on 24 August MacDonald accepted the King's commission to head a 'national' administration; and that once he had done so, he showed no such desire to renounce the position as would have been consistent with the idea of his original reluctance.

Chapter 7: 'The echo that was MacDonald': the MacDonald-Baldwin Governments, 1931–7

Theoretically the National Government was set up solely to get the country through the immediate crisis. Though this was never satisfactorily defined, it certainly meant balancing the budget and ending the run on the pound, through expenditure economies and the restoration of 'confidence'. MacDonald's first 'National' Cabinet was thus an emergency construction, half the size of a normal Cabinet, with the explicit expectation of a return to normal party politics at the ensuing general election. For MacDonald, this could only have meant the end of his political career. There was no prospect of him resuming his position in the Labour Party. He also insisted that he had not gone over to the Tories or the Liberals. *I am afraid I am not a machine-made politician, and never will be,* he explained to one Labour MP, and announced that his decision meant his political death.[1] Labour believed he had hatched a conspiracy to rescue his career. MacDonald's defence was that he was sacrificing it to the greater good.

If the hard evidence is inconclusive, the circumstantial evidence supports the Labour view. The National Government survived until 1940, winning two general elections. MacDonald, who fought for the first of them, remained its leader until June 1935. Even then he remained in the Cabinet as Lord President of the Council. Whatever the terms of the crisis, they were no longer the ones on which MacDonald had broken with his colleagues. The gold standard was abandoned within weeks of the government's formation. The introduction of tariffs, with the Ottawa agreements of September 1932, provoked the resignations from the Cabinet of Snowden and two free-trade Liberals. What remained, as MacDonald himself was acutely aware, was a party administration with himself at the head. Before the Ottawa resignations he implored his departing colleagues to consider his personal situation. *As the head of a party government ... I should be regarded as a limpet in office.*[2] This is precisely what he was.

As the head of a party government ... I should be regarded as a limpet in office.
MACDONALD

The roots of his predicament lay in the election that secured him the premiership. Baldwin's Tories, though ready to support MacDonald, were eager to do battle with Labour. By the end of September 1931 MacDonald himself believed it necessary to seek a mandate from the country. His personal role in the election was crucial; except among Labour households his prestige was never higher, and even Conservative election addresses were twice as likely to mention him as Baldwin.[3]

On the other hand, the very scale of MacDonald's victory underlined his ultimate dispensability. In breaking with Labour, he had shown little concern to rally those within the party who might have shared his views. He did not even attend the meeting of the parliamentary party called to discuss his conduct. A desperate effort was made to run a National Labour slate independent of the Conservative Party, and 35 candidates were initially projected. In the event, only 20 actually stood, of whom the 13 allowed a free run by the

Tories were successful. All seven denied it were not. The Liberals, while more than maintaining their parliamentary strength, were also disproportionately dependent on 'Liberal National' candidates depending on similar arrangements.

The underlying meaning of the 1931 election was thus of Britain's return to a two-party model of electoral competition. 'National' in reality signified anti-socialist, in the manner of the Tory-Liberal pacts that were common in local elections. In some 470 seats, government candidates faced either no opposition or a straight fight against Labour, occasionally enlivened by a fringe candidate. The result for Labour was calamitous. On one side of the house, the denuded opposition benches contained just 52 Labour MPs, even including unendorsed candidates and the ILP. Spilling over opposite was the phalanx of the 'nation', eleven times as strong, and with Liberal and Labour nationals surrounded by the highest number of Tories (also 470) ever elected. Conservatives often comported themselves as if they held the title to the nation; the National Governments of the 1930s were just the most brazen expression of that claim. Labour thus experienced its first national electoral setback since its formation. Its share of the vote, on the other hand, was almost identical with that on which MacDonald had formed his first government in 1924.[4] Labour in defeat stood as the only significant alternative to the Tories.

For MacDonald it was a strange fulfilment. In his early parliamentary career he had set out his stall against coalition government and rebuffed approaches to join a Liberal Cabinet. *I like to think*, he told the Commons in 1910, *that a day will come when we shall have two great parties – a party standing for the status quo and a party standing for progress on well-defined lines – standing for the opposition of certain principles which when they are applied to our social life will change fundamentally that social*

The special relationship?

When MacDonald visited the USA in the autumn of 1929, he was the first British Prime Minister to make the trip in an official capacity. With hindsight he thus appears as a harbinger of the 'special relationship' and MacDonald's collected American Speeches (1930) are full of references to historical ties, fellow-feeling and common interests. Nevertheless, hindsight, as so often, can be deceptive. The occasion for MacDonald's visit was Anglo-American naval rivalry and what was at stake was Britain's traditional supremacy at sea. Rapturously received, MacDonald set great store by the personal rapport he established with the US president, Herbert Hoover. *'So long as we conduct our negotiations by correspondence over thousands of miles of sea, we shall never understand each other at all'*, he addressed the American Senate. *'But in these democratic days, when heart speaks to heart as deep speaks to deep and silence talks to silence, personality, personal contact, exchange of views by the lips, sitting at two sides of a fireplace, as it was my privilege to do this weekend with your President – these things are to be as important as anything else in laying the foundation of an enduring peace all over the world.'* [*American Speeches* (Cape, London: 1930), p 30] Probably MacDonald, like some of his successors, rather flattered himself on the cosy reciprocity of the presidential ranch or fireside. Realpolitik, however, suggests a different pattern of relations, and the negotiations which followed showed that Hoover and his negotiators were no mere creatures of sentiment. David Marquand in his biography of MacDonald describes the visit as a 'milestone in America's hesitant emergence as a world power' [Marquand, *Ramsay MacDonald* (Cape, London: 1976) p 507]. Though this was less clear to MacDonald's British public, the ensuing naval agreement of 1930 was just as much a milestone in Britain's gradual relinquishment of such a position. Perhaps it was a harbinger of the special relationship after all.

life.[5] Now the two parties clearly existed, and MacDonald was at the head of the wrong one.

In some ways it was the sort of situation he must have dreamt of. At last he was disencumbered of any specific programmatic commitments, having gone to the country on the famous 'doctor's mandate' of 1931. He was also disencumbered of any burdens of parliamentary management, which Baldwin saw to with considerable skill and commendable loyalty. Nevertheless, having foresworn the party machine, and the obligations that this involved, MacDonald found himself the prisoner of his Tory majority. Not only was this a moral embarrassment, as he conceded in his diaries, it also involved a clear breach of trust with the electorate, to whom he had explicitly disavowed any intention of a party administration.

Within the Cabinet, his position at first looked much stronger. The initial allocation of four National Labour members was wholly disproportionate to the group's parliamentary strength. However, Snowden's departure then diminished it; Thomas's presence did the same, and he was to meet his end in 1936 over the alleged leaking of budget secrets. Apart from the Lord Chancellor, MacDonald's one obvious nominee in his own Cabinet was the Tory socialite Lord Londonderry, whom he preferred on personal rather than political grounds. As at last he prepared his own departure, his main stipulation was that his son Malcolm be found a place in the Cabinet. Like Lloyd George and his so-called 'family party', MacDonald in the end had nobody else he could fall back on.

Nor, it should be said, had he leadership resources of his own. When Lloyd George took on a similar role in 1916, it was as a *tour de force* of personal government, impatient of routine and always on the lookout for new sources of ideas. His deputy and parliamentary manager, Andrew Bonar Law, had to function as a sort of sounding-board to filter out the workable ideas from the unworkable ones.

There was no need for that with MacDonald and Baldwin. As always, MacDonald had little to offer domestically, where once again the dominant figure was his Chancellor, now Neville Chamberlain. Perhaps MacDonald believed that his own influence helped to mitigate the harsher aspects of Conservative philosophy. If so, he was deluding himself. Chamberlain himself combined Snowden's parsimonious instincts with a record of social reform both in his native Birmingham and as health minister. Baldwin contributed a note of emollient paternalism. Labour, even in opposition, helped to concentrate their minds rather more effectively than discredited former champions in the government itself. Where MacDonald had genuine anxieties was over the harsher aspects of unemployed relief and the means test. He was particularly concerned over its impact on the family. However, when at the beginning of 1935 Chamberlain introduced a rationalised system threatening existing scales of benefit, it was opposition in the country, including the militant opposition that MacDonald

The reputation of Neville Chamberlain (1869–1940) will be forever affected by the accusations of 'appeasement' of Hitler over the Sudetenland Crisis in 1938, which lead to the infamous Munich Agreement. Succeeding Baldwin as Prime Minister in 1937, whether his policy towards the Dictators was an attempt to buy time for rearmament, or a genuine effort to prevent war, is still debatable. His declaration of war on Nazi Germany on 3 September 1939 was a bitter admission of personal failure. He resigned on 10 May 1940 after his majority in the House of Commons was fatally cut on a vote of confidence over the Norwegian débâcle. (See *Chamberlain* by Graham Macklin, in this series.)

so deplored, that forced a retreat. What Chamberlain lacked was humanity; what Baldwin lacked was initiative. Equally in both cases, MacDonald had neither the skill nor the authority to make up the deficiency.

In foreign affairs he again cut a better figure. His Foreign Secretary was the National Liberal, Sir John Simon, who must have been suited for something, but not this. MacDonald, though, was more in his element. From the Lausanne reparations conference in June–July 1932 to the Stresa conference in April 1935, he continued to lead important British delegations. In the summer of 1933, he also presided over the abortive world economic conference held in London. Nevertheless, he discharged these responsibilities with diminishing effectiveness, in a world increasingly hostile to the ideals of conciliation for which

The desires of years had been fulfilled & I do not mind much what is to come.

MACDONALD

he stood. Already in the first months of the National Government, this was signalled by the Japanese attack on Manchuria. The following summer, Lausanne appeared to have settled the issue that had most bedevilled international relations since the war. MacDonald described it as at last a *new world. The desires of years had been fulfilled & I do not mind much what is to come.*[6] If it was a new world, MacDonald deserved much of the credit.

But of course what was to come was Hitler; the new world had arrived too late. This was least of all MacDonald's doing, and by the end of his life he was coming to have strong reservations about the appeasement of fascism, notably in Spain. What he lacked was the resolution to give effect such misgivings. At the Stresa conference with France and Italy, he had the opportunity to raise with Mussolini what he knew to be Italy's indefensible attack on Abyssinia. He did not choose to do so, however; the resulting communiqué confined itself expressly to the 'peace of Europe'.

Now approaching 70, MacDonald was a somewhat pathetic figure. His performances in the Commons were unconvincing and sometimes incoherent. His former colleague J R Clynes, who was anything but malicious, described him in his memoirs as 'the echo that was MacDonald'. An unkind but not inaccurate observer recorded how 'things ... got to the stage when nobody knew what the Prime Minister was going to say in the House of Commons, and, when he did say it, nobody understood it'.[7] MacDonald was fully aware of his deteriorating powers. His note of lachrymose self-pity became accentuated, and the note of hypochondria exacerbated and legitimised by the glaucoma for which he was treated in 1932.

For some he became a figure of fun. A young Tory, Bob Boothby, described meeting MacDonald by the lake in Lausanne and winding him up with the observation that he looked very well. *To tell you the truth I am absolutely rotten*, MacDonald confided tragically. 'Then a lot of stage work. Head in the hands, etc. Hardly ever slept without drugs. Awful strain. Especially having to do Chamberlain's work (a most frightful lie). Eyes giving way (they are much better). Heart giving way. Mind giving way. Doubted if he could carry on much longer... . He wailed and wailed about the Labour party and Conservative party and the Press and the weather and the House of Commons ... until I wondered whether to push him in the water and throw stones at him, or try to smother him with a handkerchief. What a man.'[8]

Denied the customary prop of party, and the creature of his ostensible subordinates, MacDonald's descent from one-man government was precipitous. Reginald Bassett, an advocate of his cause, described his predicament as anomalous and degrading.[9] There can hardly have been a weaker Prime Minister, nor one held in such little regard by supporters and opponents alike.

Though few talked more than MacDonald of their weariness of office, it needed the build-up of pressure from within the Conservative Party to bring matters to a head in the early part of 1935. The timetable he then agreed with Baldwin was revealing of his priorities. *I asked him to assume that I might have to give up the Premiership this year but on no account before the Jubilee ceremonies & not before the India Bill was on the Statute Book*, MacDonald reported after a preliminary discussion in February 1935. The first condition he held to: George V's Silver Jubilee celebrations of early May provided glittering ceremonial and streets lined with admirers. When the King invited MacDonald to stand with him before the vast cheering crowd, he enjoyed what by now was a rare sense of elation and perhaps a fitting moment at which to bow out. He resigned in favour of Baldwin on 7 June. The India Bill, forgotten, went onto the statute book on 4 August.

Remaining in the Cabinet, MacDonald took the brave decision to stand again at Seaham at the 1935 general election. Rejected by a margin of more than two to one, he then allowed himself to be manoeuvred back into Parliament for one of the university constituencies whose plural votes he had always opposed. The beneficiary of considerable Conservative arm-twisting, he was nominated by the Association of Unionist Graduates and won the seat. He finally retired from the Cabinet when Baldwin resigned as Prime Minister in May 1937. Enough of his old independence remained for him to decline the offer of a peerage. Six months later, on 9 November 1937, he died *en route* for a holiday in South America. He was buried alongside his wife at Spynie, Morayshire, where the journey had begun.

Part Three

THE LEGACY

Chapter 8: No Possible Posterity? Ramsay MacDonald in Retrospect

Considered as a 20th-century prime minister, MacDonald's reputation presents a paradox. From when Salisbury saw out the previous century, to when Blair saw in the next, he stands with Asquith, Baldwin, Churchill, Wilson and Thatcher as one of Britain's longest-serving Prime Ministers. To link his name with theirs nevertheless underlines how little positive impression his actions in government made. Even Baldwin, with whom his name is often coupled, is identifiable with a distinct political period and the style of government which he brought to it. As much as anything, it was one defined by the challenge of Labour and the new mass democracy which MacDonald himself personified. Baldwin's career, at least domestically, stands for the successful accommodation of these pressures. One of the ironies of MacDonald's is the extent to which even his own nominal leadership falls beneath this Baldwinian shadow. When Labour returned to office in 1945, there were some who could see it as inheriting the mantle of great reforming Liberal governments of the past. But as far as Labour itself was concerned, it began with virtually a clean slate.

There were extenuating circumstances. Economically, MacDonald's were seven lean years, not fat ones. Politically, only James Callaghan enjoyed so little of the parliamentary majority which British Prime Ministers have usually been able to count upon. Even that is not quite accurate; for MacDonald during the greater part of his premiership presided over what formally speaking was an unassailable parliamentary majority. He did so, however, not as its architect and recognised leader, but as its prisoner. Lloyd George and possibly Churchill, superficially his nearest counterparts, were both installed as national leaders through the support of political opponents and at the expense of normal party calculations. Both, however, enjoyed immense personal authority as war leaders, in periods when party constraints and loyalties were subordinated to a larger national purpose. Churchill even reversed the normal progressions of office in attaining the leadership of his party only as a by-product of his elevation to the leadership of the country. All three of these leaders were preoccupied with foreign affairs; for the other two, this was what had brought them to office in such unusual circumstances. MacDonald's crisis of 1931, in comparison, was a weak pretext for coalition, just as the 'national' administration to which it gave rise was a dubious form of emergency government. Nothing showed that better than its demise: for when, in 1940, genuine national crisis demanded a more authentic national government, the *ersatz* version of MacDonald-Baldwin-Chamberlain collapsed ignominiously.

Not even Lloyd George did as much as MacDonald to alienate his own party. Even he had the satisfaction of observing how little the Liberals could flourish without him. Again, while all these three leaders spent years in the political wilderness, MacDonald's alone were the ones he spent in the highest office. Unlike even Chamberlain and Eden, whose reputations were similarly damaged by the exercise of that office, he was unique in having exercised no ministerial functions except as Prime Minister. Nor, unlike Chamberlain, had he any significant experience in local government. His reputation as a constructive politician rests on his premiership alone. He had a mixed but not discreditable record in foreign affairs. Otherwise, there is almost nothing to be said for it. The most that even his defenders offer is that others would not have done much better.

His accomplishments, whatever one makes of them, were of a rather different order; and they tell us a good deal about the curious circumvolutions of this age of political confusion and realignment. On the one hand, MacDonald demands consideration as the consummate political strategist who contributed as much as anybody to the one tectonic shift in the British party system over the last 160 years. At once an orator, a publicist, an organiser and a political thinker, MacDonald as a party leader symbolised Labour's new political standing and its gradual displacement of the ailing Liberal tradition with which he and his party had such a love-hate relationship. Here MacDonald provides the straight narrative thread of a purposeful party career, one which Labour would certainly have celebrated had it not been for the events of 1931. In a thoughtful essay, Trevor Lloyd has commented that Mac-Donald's importance in British political history depends at least as much on these activities as on anything he did while leading the country. If his record as Prime Minister appears as an 'anti-climax', this was a measure of his achievement in getting there as well as of his limitations in office.[1]

By the same token, the sense of anti-climax also derived from expectations of where Labour was meant to be heading, and how it might have used its hold on government to get there. Unlike Baldwin or Bonar Law, a Labour Prime Minister invites judgement as a political reformer; and it is on this basis least of all that a case can be made for MacDonald. What he provided was not the radicalism which Labour's emergence had appeared to portend, but a Baldwinian instinct of 'safety first' that was more deeply embedded in his own political philosophy than his embrace of socialism might suggest. Baldwinian eventually in the literal sense of depending on Baldwin himself, it was nevertheless through the Labour Party that MacDonald best served Baldwinian goals of tempering the feared excesses of the new mass democracy. Avowedly a socialist but with a collectivist liberal programme, he was also deeply conservative in his beliefs regarding the nature of authority and the preconditions of good government. With the bemusement of an outsider, Egon Wertheimer observed in 1929 that while Baldwin was temperamentally a Liberal, and Lloyd George a typical socialist, MacDonald alone of the main party leaders was fundamentally a Conservative.[2] It would have been truer to say that he was something of all three. MacDonald, at least, is the only British Prime Minister that might have sat in Cabinets dominated by any of the parties – and very nearly did.

Eventually the compact failed to hold. In an age of real social tension, MacDonald became a deeply divisive figure, as much loathed by his opponents as Thatcher, but without the countervailing devotion of the Conservative nation. As he rightly reflected at the stop of the stairs at Londonderry House, he was to have no posterity. If he nevertheless maintained a precarious balance between these conflicting elements for so long, this was not merely a sign of the temporary fluidity between the parties. What distinguished MacDonald from

We need the 'professional politician' just as much as we need the professional engineer, or the professional doctor, or the professional chimney sweep. The art and science of government is one of the most difficult of all the arts and sciences, and care should be taken to enable it to command the most skilled intelligences.

MACDONALD

less favoured contemporaries were the skills and sense of vocation of the new breed of professional politician of whom he was in many ways an archetype. From Lossiemouth to Londonderry House he was a performer, and it was in performance alone that he excelled.

It was also in this performance of the art of leadership that he made his career – not as a matter of birthright but as the profession of which he had made himself master. *We need the 'professional politician' just as much as we need the professional engineer, or the professional doctor, or the professional chimney sweep*, he wrote after his first entry into Parliament. *The art and science of government is one of the most difficult of all the arts and sciences, and care should be taken to enable it to command the most skilled intelligences*.[3] Later he used more high-flown language, describing his role as that of the *craftsman creator ... moulding human affairs so that as the generations end he may be able to survey his work and feel that it is good and is evolving according to a desirable plan*.[4] It is as a craftsman creator that his career may be evaluated.

People and aristocracy
For activists and supporters, the initial wonder of a Labour government lay not so much in what it did as what it was. 'There sat side by side,' a backbencher recalled of the party's arrival in office, 'teachers, bricklayers, dockers, shop assistants, colliers and cotton operatives, occupying the places of the mighty. It seemed as of the work of generations had been completed in less than a quarter of a century...'[5] In the writings of Keir Hardie, who personified this conception of labour representation, it had sometimes been expounded even to the exclusion of leadership by the 'so-called intellectual classes'. More typically, by the time of the first Labour government, the claim was made of representing all useful sections

of society. MacDonald himself described the Parliamentary Labour Party as *the most complete representation of national thought and experience that sits in any corner of the House*.[6] The inclusion of several peers in his first government, which for its leader connoted a still broader basis of representation, was held by supporters to reflect only the 'peculiar circumstances' of its minority status. The real significance of a Labour Cabinet, wrote Molly Hamilton, was its experience of workers' conditions of life 'from the inside'. 'Most of them were born into poverty, and escaped from it, where they have escaped, by their own exertions, backed by an exceptional endowment of brains and character.' Genuine representatives, they knew to the full what the 'prison-house of circumstance' meant for Labour's supporters.[7]

Such credentials were a precondition for leading the early Labour Party. As Hamilton recorded in the first biography of MacDonald, 'none of our conquerors ever started with the material odds heavier against him'; his background was one of 'dire poverty'.[8] In the *Herald Book of Labour Members*, like an inversion of Burke's *Landed Peerage*, 'Scottish peasant parents' confirmed his authenticity of lineage. Along with the Scottish accent which MacDonald refined but never relinquished, his origins in Lossiemouth remained a very public component of his identity. In the journalistic sketches he collected as *Wanderings and Excursions* (1925) and *At Home and Abroad* (1936), evocations of his Scottish origins figured prominently. Lossiemouth, according to another of his early biographers, Godfrey Elton, was a 'grim little village of fisherfolk and farmworkers', lashed by the rain, buffeted by screaming winds, threatened by the grey menace of the firth.[9] MacDonald himself liked to evoke *the Viking wrath* of the elements, like a test of fortitude and human endurance. *Thatch and slates fly, chimney pots smash, sheds are unroofed, but the huddled abodes stand by each other ...*

threatened but unconquered.[10] Cynics predicted, wrongly, that he would end his career as the Earl of Lossiemouth. But the point about Lossiemouth was that this was not his title but his birthright.

Like so much else in MacDonald's career, however, the connection was not all that it seemed. Possibly its very ambivalence provides a clue to MacDonald's character. Though Lossiemouth linked him with a notion of the common people, this was not at all the urban proletariat on which both actually and symbolically Labour's advance had so greatly depended. Instead, it represented for MacDonald the ideal of a rugged independence, more at war with nature than with an exploiting class. As we shall see, it was the antithesis of everything he identified with the modern city. *The folk earn their scanty living amidst danger and hardship on the waters, and they are willing that it should be so*, he wrote of the unspoilt fishing community:

They are not tended, fed, pruned and sheltered like the flowers of a garden. They are comely people of easy dignity of carriage like all men and women unburdened by the spirit of servitude and living a life of natural independence.[11]

Located at the periphery, beyond the experience of most of his readers, the images had an almost fabulous quality, like the evocations of North America or Ceylon with which his publishers collected them. As Marquand notes, his Scottishness, or at least his rural Scottishness, only made it harder to place him. Like Lloyd George of Llanystumdwy, MacDonald seemed to occupy an indeterminate position beyond or perhaps predating the categories of the modern class system.

Rather than the collective action of the unions or co-operatives, formative radical influences were linked with the countryside and a tradition of individualism. It was not unusual for a socialist of MacDonald's generation that the land reformer Henry George should have been one of these influences. In his later socialist writings, the issue of the land, as of rent, was to retain a prominent place and the 'servility' of the English shires was contrasted with the fearless independence of the Scot. MacDonald also stressed the bias towards communal ownership that was particularly marked in Scotland.[12] Bereft of ideas to meet the unemployment crisis, it was characteristic that he should have stressed the idea of rural resettlement. In 1930 he did so to a sceptical Labour conference. *There is a case where you take men – I do not mean their bodies only, but their minds and souls – off the pavements which have no roots and no rootable capacity, and put them in the fields, where they till and grow and sow and harvest.* (A voice: 'And Starve.') ... *It may not be luxurious, but it is healthy, and I wish there were some more of us sticking to that rough, humble fare than there are in these somewhat degenerate days...* [13]

For MacDonald himself, issues of proprietorship may have been less important than that of access. One story about him is that on visits back to Lossiemouth he would take his children on a ceremonial trespass across the property of the local laird, cutting through barbed-wire fences as an initiation into that spirit of independence. His own appetite for walking was legendary and he suggested that even the Conservative who enjoyed the open country sensed the immorality of an individual claiming ownership of it. One of the few times in the Commons that he unequivocally supported direct action was in connection with an Access to Mountains Bill. *He was one of those who delighted in trespassing*, he ventured, no doubt to the 'oohs!' of the benches

In Scotland the feeling still remains common amongst the people that private property in land is on a totally different footing to private property in anything else, that trespass is no illegality, that poaching either for rabbit or trout, is no crime, and that access to mountains is a common right

MACDONALD

opposite. *He had been there without permission and he proposed to go again without permission.*[14] Combining ideas of communal rights and individual protest, this perhaps represented his most deep-seated objection to private ownership. As he put it in 1921, *in Scotland the feeling still remains common amongst the people that private property in land is on a totally different footing to private property in anything else, that trespass is no illegality, that poaching either for rabbit or trout, is no crime, and that access to mountains is a common right.*[15]

In the Commons debate on access MacDonald introduced another curious accent which helps to reconcile what seem the contradictory aspects of his character. In theory, of course, MacDonald argued that the economic foundations of a landed aristocracy were passing, and that it was the task of socialists to hasten the process on. On the other hand, he could not resist offering a favourable comparison between what he called the *real aristocracy* and the more stringent approach to access questions of the *nouveaux riches*. This was not the only such occasion. In the 'Peers against the People' debates, though MacDonald proposed the abolition of the Lords, he offered similar reflections in defence of what he called the fox-hunting classes. *On the shoulders of our ancient aristocracy tippets hang naturally, and the coronets sit quite naturally upon their brows, but on the shoulders of our newer nobility, of those who have just left holiday-making on Blackpool sands, the tippets do not hang naturally.* Some might have wondered what a tippet was. Anybody might have wondered how one could hang naturally. MacDonald, however, had a regard for the traditional appurtenances of authority that was almost fetishistic in character. As he conceded in the Commons, he was *one of those curious specimens of a Conservative who sits with the Labour party. I am Conservative because I have a profound respect for historical institutions.*[16]

Evidently this foreshadowed the MacDonald who in 1924 disconcerted many supporters by the avidity with which he embraced the ceremonial aspects of his position. Seduced by the aesthetics of privilege, his political resistances, as we have seen, were to prove wholly inadequate. Inseparable from this, and no less significant, was the shudder of revulsion at the thought of Blackpool sands. The impression MacDonald gave was of distaste for plebeians at play as well as plutocrats, indeed for plutocrats precisely because they were really plebeians. This was to be a consistent motif. From the late Victorian penny press to the American films he described as sickening, MacDonald deplored the new mass culture of the times and regarded the *dependence of the public for recreation, entertainment, religion and ideals upon the monied classes ... [as] lowering the tone of democratic opinion and the character of democratic ideals ...*[17] Symptomatic was his approval of the high-minded paternalism of his fellow Scot John Reith, who in 1922 became general manager of the British Broadcasting Company (as the BBC then was). *Keep up the standard*, MacDonald wrote to him the following year. *Do not play down. Remember that the great mass of our people really want good things.*[18]

In 1922 John Reith (1889–1971) became general manager of the British Broadcasting Company, the first radio broadcaster in Britain, and when it was transformed into the British Broadcasting Corporation, funded by the licence fee, by royal charter in 1927, he became its first Director-General, serving until 1938. The BBC's 'Reithian' ethos to 'inform, educate and entertain' was established by him, and it held a monopoly of broadcasting in Britain until 1952. The first regular BBC television broadcasts began in November 1936, but they were suspended on the outbreak of the Second World War in September 1939.

The democratic ideal of independence was thus confused in MacDonald's mind with values and associations that set it apart from the common crowd. One of them, again, was that of aristocracy. *They are the stout stems of a natural aristocracy*, he wrote of the Lossiemouth fisherfolk, *equalitarian in all the essentials of spirit and bearing without being servile and doing reverence without being sycophantic.*[19] MacDonald himself cultivated exactly such a bearing and perhaps did not greatly mind if he was mistaken for the real thing. 'It is so plain from his distinguished head, his address, his rings, that he is not a TU leader, but an aristocrat', a close observer noted in 1926.[20] 'J R M is *not* a snob, but he genuinely prefers the aristocrat to the proletarian as everyday associates', said the Earl de la Warr.[21] Society gossip by this time had even turned to the

'J R M *is* not *a snob, but he genuinely prefers the aristocrat to the proletarian as everyday associates',*

EARL DE LA WARR

patrician identity of his father, as the Duchess of Sutherland beamed to her sister that 'MacDonald is no Labour man, he is one of us'.[22] She was among those whose hospitality to MacDonald was eventually to be thought so corrupting.

A Highland identity was thus in itself of some ambiguity. Its connection with Lossiemouth, technically not even in the Highlands, was more problematic still: for the world which MacDonald evoked was changing, and changing apace. Linked up to the national railway system, with a population that doubled in the 40 years after his birth, Lossiemouth by the end of the century was a resort as well as a fishing village. The younger women had laid aside their lobster baskets for their rail fare out. Title deeds were in the hands of the moneylender. The old boats were museum pieces and even the independent seafarer was now a hired servant. Worst of all, MacDonald wrote in 1913, the villages of the firth were being *absorbed in the world. Ichabod was written over them when the flood of summer visitors came with all the airs of the 'Sooth Countree'* ...[23] Again, there was a flavour at once of upstart plutocracy and the Blackpool seafront. MacDonald in his journalism described the new incursions as a deluge and invasion, of ugly little bungalows and a *leprous pink covering of abominations*, ruining the landscape of his early years. *Where we played 'the bat', there are hotels. Where we went bird-nesting, there are 'greens' ... the Goths have invaded us.*[24]

The paradox remained. Despite the elegiac tone, MacDonald himself not only caught the train out of Lossiemouth, but was one of the crowd that each year came flooding back. Though he did so, he said, to commune with the elements and departed spirits, he was not above mixing with Goths on the golf course. Indeed, this was a more significant part of his identity than its public projections might suggest. Where golf in MacDonald's youth had been played an open land, the famous 'greens' were now established of the Moray Golf Club, like a modern form of enclosure. Clubhouses were built in 1893 and 1900, and expanded in 1923 when Molly Hamilton described the village as 'one of the Scottish golf paradises'. Naturally, the club website makes little of mists and gales: the climate is 'remarkably favourable', the rainfall exceptionally low and golf is often played on every day of the year.

MacDonald could have dreamt of nothing better. Walking and golf were the two recreations he mentioned in his *Who's Who* entry. The first of them provided a public face that was brooding, romantic, introspective. The second provided a private face that was companionable, domesticated, suburban. Like Lossiemouth itself, golf combined a more popular Scottish ethos with points of entry into the establishment through one of its most debilitating fads. Already in 1896, when MacDonald warned his future wife that he could have *nothing whatever to do with a girl who cannot swing a golf club*, he did so between rounds with a *dignified Dean* and *a Professor of Church History*.[25] Appropriately, he even evoked the sort of Calvinistic spirit that one sometimes finds identified with his upbringing. Losing a game against his old schoolmaster, he told how he insisted on seeing out the game in pouring rain and emerged victorious – a true example of justification by faith. *The dear old man when we left the last hole put his hand in mine and with a lump in his throat said 'MacDonald, when I saw you first as a fat little boy I said you were either doomed to be hanged or something worth doing. Our game tonight has me feel once again a babe in your hands.' I am telling you that because I really think he was right.*[26]

There are far too many people about now who are just out for a quiet living on an income provided by the State and one of these days some Government will have to put its foot down.

MACDONALD

A study of this sub-plot would be worth undertaking. Beatrice Webb in 1913 was scornful of MacDonald's cementing of a Lib-Lab relations over games of golf with Liberal leaders. 'Imagine a German Social Democratic leader playing golf with the German Prime Minister! The British governing class is extraordinarily clever in winning over the abler revolutionary elements!'[27] Three years later, MacDonald's hurt at being expelled from the Lossiemouth club left a bitter sense of rejection and dispossession, and his allegiance shifted irrevocably to Spey Bay just up the coast. It was here that in 1924 he invited General Thomson for the discussion that helped shape his first Cabinet. It was here that he invited Cecily Gordon-Cumming in one of his platonic liaisons of the 1920s. It was from here too that in the run-up to the 1935 election he offered Baldwin his reflections on the economy, having met *a lot of interesting people knocking about ... a couple of bank managers who are up here ...* [and] *a stockbroker who is in the city.* His view of the current unemployment scales with which one may be sure they concurred: *There are far too many people about now who are just out for a quiet living on an income provided by the State and one of these days some Government will have to put its foot down.*[28] Like Burnham Wood, the 'Sooth' had came to Lossiemouth. The rugged independence of the fisherfolk had given way to the glib intolerance of 'doles' of the suburban golfer.

Focus of the hopes of a whole class

Little of this figured in MacDonald's public persona. Instead, his effectiveness as a Labour leader was that he fulfilled the movement's need for symbolic representation, as a sort of projection of its collective self, but at the same time provided the charisma and disinterestedness of the traditional radical platform. According to Joe Clayton, whose association with MacDonald went back to the 1890s, his advancement within the labour movement reflected the preference of working people for the leadership of a 'gentleman' in whom all trace of his lowly birth was now expunged.[29] In reality, a gentleman pure and simple could not have conveyed so effectively Labour's claims to representation, and would hardly at this stage have been chosen to do so. Wertheimer noted the 'proletarian snobbery' which eased the passage of the well-born within the Labour Party. He also wondered how this could be reconciled with the proletarian self-respect which was no less strikingly exhibited by the British working class. MacDonald, with his ambiguous status, seemed to reconcile them perfectly. Like Lenin, he was an almost legendary being, 'the focus of the mute hopes of a whole class'.[30]

How strange that a German social democrat should have

been struck by this resemblance to a Russian revolutionary cult exploiting highly traditional attitudes to personal authority. Robert Michels in his classic *Political Parties* was another astute German observer who noticed the more personalised character of socialist leadership in Britain. Weaker than is often imagined in respect of its organisational resources, the rise of British Labour depended on a charismatic style of leadership that served both as a projection of mute aspirations, and perhaps as compensation for their deferment. Keir Hardie again provided an exemplar, and according to the Clydesider Patrick Dollan it was on MacDonald that Hardie's mantle fell after his death in 1915. Another was William Gladstone, and Dollan also described MacDonald as 'the Gladstone of Labour', the unconquerable leader of the suppressed and suffering.[31]

Nourishing his children from a milk jug bearing Gladstone's portrait, MacDonald was grounded in this culture and familiar with its expectations.[32] It meant in some sense remaining of the 'people', including the activist element on which the labour movement depended for its voluntary workers. But it also required sufficient detachment from these activists to assure both elites and a wider electoral constituency of Labour's fitness to exercise traditional forms of authority. The balance between these conflicting elements was inherently an unstable one. Perhaps they were most effectively synthesised on MacDonald's triumphal electoral tour of 1924, when the cautious exercise of national office combined with the renewed enmity of a red-scare press to underline his appeal as a leader risen from the masses. Underlying such grand spectacles, however, a growing disjuncture between the two elements was to culminate in the choice between 'country' and 'party' which MacDonald had to make in 1931. Ironically, it was the reaction to his defection that as much as anything helped establish a collective labourist ethos through which these tensions were to some extent brought under control.

One way to trace this changing relationship is through the constituencies which MacDonald represented or sought to represent. Here one sees from the start how important was MacDonald's conception of the professional politician. With none of the six constituencies which he sought to represent did he have any meaningful prior connection. At a theoretical level, he upheld constituency representation as a form of communal expression, providing a psychological link between national affairs and the local community.[33] To this, the idea of labour representation added the notion of a wider class interest that transcended the locality and local forms of patronage. MacDonald, however, had no such record of service either through the unions or – unless one counts his brief experience of the LCC – through local political affairs. Canvassing for nominations from his London address, he was both a less affluent version of the Liberal or Tory carpetbagger and a forerunner of Labour's new breed of middle-class candidates of the inter-war years.

Even in his earliest conflicts with local Liberal caucuses, MacDonald came across very much like the metropolitan professional. In Southampton in 1894, he was initially confronted with the competition of a local pig curer named Barnes. Encountering resistance not just as a socialist – he hardly used the word – but as a 'stranger', MacDonald retaliated with 'manners' and connections: *It is no great boast to say that there is no Labour candidate before England at this moment with worse manners than those of Mr Barnes, and for myself I*

You must consider the National situation as well as the local situation; and if the loss of a seat in the South means the gain of half a dozen in the North, you have made a good bargain.

MACDONALD

*daresay I have half a dozen close middle-class and society friends for
his one.* MacDonald also suggested the sort of electoral calcu-
lation he was later to practise so assiduously: *You must consider
the National situation as well as the local situation; and if the loss
of a seat in the South means the gain of half a dozen in the North,
you have made a good bargain.*[34]

Though some things obviously changed little over the
course of MacDonald's career, at this point he had neither
the resources nor the machinery to make his claims effective.
When the Liberals eventually selected as their candidate the
president of the local trades council, it is arguable that he did
not even have the necessary working-class credentials.

Shifting his candidacy to Leicester in 1899, MacDonald at
first established a close rapport with his constituency and for
the first time emerged as a credible parliamentary champion in
Labour's cause. Nevertheless, behind the victories he achieved
in 1906 and 1910 there were inherent tensions between
Labour's aspirations locally and the strategy MacDonald was
pursuing nationally. The preconditions for his victories were
twofold and potentially contradictory. One was the establishment of a vigorous Labour Representation Committee, with
its own local paper the *Leicester Pioneer*, which MacDonald and
Henderson invoked as a model of effective organisation for
others to follow. The other, of course, was the electoral arrangement MacDonald had made with the Liberal whips. Here the
phenomenon of the two-member constituency proved a mixed
blessing, for it meant that potentially the pressure for Labour
to take the offensive against the Liberals could be exercised
even within his own constituency. Fortuitously, the issue was
brought to a head by the resignation of MacDonald's Liberal
running partner as the result of a divorce scandal in 1913.

Some have suggested that MacDonald's pre-war reputation
never recovered from the dispute which followed.[35] Opinion

within the local labour movement ran strongly in favour of contesting the resulting by-election. MacDonald himself was largely instrumental in the refusal of national endorsement for a Labour candidate. When opinion began to rally in favour of an independent socialist, he then let it be known that support for his candidacy would be regarded as an act of censure upon himself, jeopardising his commitment to the constituency. The prominence given his comments in the Liberals' election manifesto provoked a veritable furore that symbolised the gulf that now existed between MacDonald and many Labour activists. 'They sense him as being of a different class and a different type', commented one former associate, 'and, while honestly admiring, suspect his cleverness, with the result that he never has the luck to find his finger on the pulse of labour.'[36]

One would never have guessed as much when MacDonald was chosen as Aberavon's parliamentary candidate following his defeat in Leicester in 1918. The war years, as we saw, were central to the establishment of the mystique of MacDonald's leadership. In a movement steeped in Christian symbolism, the image of Gethsemane and political resurrection had a deep resonance, nowhere more so than in a Nonconformist stronghold like Aberavon. Until his death in 1915, the neighbouring seat of Merthyr had been represented by Hardie and even now the memory served to neutralise renewed Liberal objections to MacDonald as a foreigner. *Instead of Scottish being a reproach here it is a commendation*, he wrote.[37] Already on his first election in 1922, the scenes were described in the *South Wales News* as reminiscent of the great Welsh religious revival of 1904.[38]

It was in this period that the analogies with both Gladstone and Hardie came most easily, as MacDonald cemented his political authority through his mastery of the radical platform.

In both 1923 and 1924 he made triumphal election tours concluding in Aberavon. Accompanying him the second time, the journalist Henry Nevinson described how MacDonald was roundly booed by the 'parasitic population' of Malvern, as if merely to accentuated his appeal as the champion of the underdog. 'All the way through the Black Country ... MacDonald was greeted as though he were the man for whom the working people had been waiting to deliver them from their wretchedness', Nevinson recounted: 'The car could hardly move. We had to shut off the engine, and allow the crowds to push us along. The people swarmed on every inch of it, and clung to every bit of MacDonald they could touch.'[39]

'All the way through the Black Country ... MacDonald was greeted as though he were the man for whom the working people had been waiting to deliver them from their wretchedness ... The car could hardly move. We had to shut off the engine, and allow the crowds to push us along. The people swarmed on every inch of it, and clung to every bit of MacDonald they could touch.'

HENRY NEVINSON

Crowds often in their thousands gathered to witness the legendary platform style that MacDonald by this time had perfected. According to Molly Hamilton, he could range from expressive, almost cello-like cadences to the crack of a pistol, all with a beauty that was his alone. Others who heard it likened his voice to an organ: 'one of the most beautiful platform instruments of all time ... capable of every range of expression, from a whisper to the great bass notes of an organ'. Whatever it was that moved the crowds, it was not the antics of a rabble-rouser. The 'Mac' of Labour's heroic years was just as often now 'Gentleman Mac'. 'He moves on the platform with complete freedom, an easy expressive grace. There is no gesticulation, but every action suggests harmonious co-operation of brain and body.'[40]

In retrospect, the campaign appears both as one of the high points of the radical platform and as its swan-song – at least as far any mainstream party leader was concerned. Two contrasting decisions provided an augury of things to come. Labour for its part invested in the advanced technology of a powerful loudspeaker system that allowed MacDonald to hold even the largest crowds spellbound. Baldwin, on the other hand, used the still more advanced technology of the wireless to project a homely, fireside manner with consummate skill and ease. The contrast with MacDonald's muffled broadcast from a public meeting was just the first of many victories of the studio over the platform. MacDonald, who had an avid interest in the BBC, was not to slow to draw the moral. He was the first Prime Minister to install a television set at Number 10 and he became an effective radio broadcaster in his own right.

This shift in the character of political communications was to be one factor in the souring of the relationship between MacDonald and his constituency. Irrespective of the effectiveness or otherwise of the great public meeting, MacDonald now exercised significant party responsibilities at Westminster. Nurtured on the rhetoric of labour representation, supporters in Aberavon expected to see their MP regularly. Confronted with political realities which the same rhetoric sometimes overlooked, they also needed him to contribute to the constituency's running expenses. At the same time, there remained the expectation that MacDonald as Labour leader would be available as a public speaker in other parts of the country. Even though a wider electorate was beginning to be reached by the national media, within the labour movement itself the evangelist qualities of the public meeting continued to provide both inspiration and the sense of a common identity. Again it was a transitional period, and it is understandable that MacDonald should have found the multiple demands of leadership difficult to reconcile.

It is also clear that in a very real and deliberate sense he was seeking to distance himself from these old associations and responsibilities. His attendance to courtly ceremonial functions as what he called the *historical parts* of his duties may or may not have been justified on grounds of protocol. What was definitely damaging was his hunger for such connections and the corrosive effect this had on his judgement and integrity. At his first palace reception as premier, he was fatefully seated next to Lady Londonderry. No figure could have been more remote from the labour movement. The Londonderrys were leading society hosts, whose lavish receptions at their Park Lane home were a high point in the Conservative social calendar. Arriving at Londonderry House, guests attended by powdered flunkeys might take a quarter of an hour to reach the top of the great staircase, where Lady Londonderry would await with the current Conservative leader. Observers all agreed that it was like something out of another era. The sober Bonar Law was grateful to have the burden of entertaining taken off his shoulders. Baldwin, his successor, thought it a leftover from 'the golden age of corruption' and out of step with Tory democracy. Others were admitted to Lady Londonderry's private circle with the password of a nickname. 'Winston the Warlock' was one. 'Simon the Silkworm' – the future Foreign Secretary Sir John Simon – was another.

MacDonald – he was to become 'Hamish' – found it irresistible. At their first meeting, he and Lady Londonderry discovered their common identity as 'Highlanders'. A few weeks later the Londonderrys were the first guests to sign in his Chequers' visitors' book. However, it was in 1925– 6 that his taste for such connections began to provoke real tension between MacDonald and his own supporters. Partly this was because they were beyond his ordinary means and making up the difference cut into the time he had for the labour movement. Thanks to the legacy of a wealthy benefactor, MacDonald moved in late 1925 to a 20-roomed Georgian house in old Hampstead, Upper Frognal Lodge. For its new occupant, it meant removing himself from the city in both time and place. Beneath him was the *world of these days, pretentious, commonplace, crowded, formal, without personality.* But around him both Time and Death seemed to have been forgotten; he was *three minutes from the tube station and three hundred miles from London and all it stands for.*[41]

Not the least of its advantages was that it allowed him to exchange social invitations without the stigma of patronage or servility. Lord Londonderry was one of the first to receive his address. *If ever you or Lady Londonderry want a walk on Hampstead Heath on a Saturday or Sunday afternoon when I am in town, come and pick me up and return with me to tea. I am just on the edge of the Heath in a nice old Georgian house.*[42] It was thus that in the early part of 1926 MacDonald picked up the acquaintance with the Londonderrys and this time made sure to maintain it. The same year he also enjoyed long holidays in Ceylon and the Sahara. His Aberavon mining constituents enjoyed a six-month lockout.

Whether wisely or not, as he admitted, he had added £300 a year to his living expenses, when the basic parliamentary salary was only £400.[43] Speaking engagements, by convention, involved no fee. Journalism therefore remained an important source of income. In 1925 he even stipulated a fee for contributions to the ILP's *Socialist Review*. Between his political responsibilities, his social commitments and the income he now required to live on, MacDonald found the labour movement contacts on which his career had been built increasingly tiresome. In 1926 he published a letter in the *Daily Herald* requesting not to be sent speaking invitations by local Labour parties. When they did arrive he insisted his Sundays had to be devoted to making an income. His papers for that year are full of refusals of possible Sunday meetings: *You imagine that we have got nothing to except come on platforms and talk – no House of Commons work that requires preparation, no work required for bread and cheese, no rest and no recreation*, he told one importunate local socialist.[44] Understandably, in adopting a not dissimilar attitude to his supporters in Aberavon he caused considerable ill-feeling.

What he needed was a pocket borough. The best that Labour could offer was a Durham miners' seat, and in 1929 MacDonald shifted his candidacy to Seaham. No subscriptions were required, nor need he visit more than once a year; the pressures of his office were fully understood. MacDonald took them at their word. Coincidentally, the major coalowner in the district was Lord Londonderry, and the Londonderrys alone continued to receive the assiduous attentions denied his other constituents. It helped provide a fitting epitaph to his personal history of labour representation when his constituency party disowned him in 1931. Standing against him in the ensuing election was his own agent, a local miner, and MacDonald scented the real possibility of defeat. *Labour I am and Labour I shall remain*, he declaimed defiantly on the hustings. But he also wrote to Lady Londonderry in the excruciating style they affected in their correspondence: *My Dear Ladye, do see that your following vote. This is looking an ominous thing at the moment*.[45] In the event, he secured a majority of nearly 6,000.

At last it was MacDonald's turn at the head of the stairs at Londonderry House. It even provided an incongruous setting for National Labour's first big reception. David Marquand's view is that friendships like Lady Londonderry's made no difference to MacDonald's political behaviour. Others saw it differently. The Tory F E Smith had once described Londonderry as 'catering his way to the Cabinet'. He made it there successfully in 1931, as MacDonald's choice as Secretary for Air. Baldwin was convinced that the Londonderrys' friendship for MacDonald was motivated by rank ambition. Londonderry himself, with thanks to his wife, described himself as 'Ramsay's man'. But by this time he was one of the few.

The socialism of Ramsay MacDonald

To Beatrice Webb the MacDonald of the 1920s was not a socialist and had not been one for 20 years. Rather, she thought him 'a mild radical with individualist leanings and aristocratic tastes'.[46] Everything MacDonald did in government seemed to confirm it; nothing he initiated bore the specific hallmark of socialism. On the other hand, such an assessment seems impossible to reconcile with his activities outside Parliament. Unique among British prime ministers in the extent to which he expounded his social philosophy, between 1905 and 1921 MacDonald published around a dozen books dealing with social and political issues. These covered such diverse topics as India, militarism and the labour unrest, but in the majority of cases were expressly concerned with the exposition of socialism and socialist policy. To them one might add MacDonald's prolific output of socialist journalism and editorial initiatives like the ILP journal the *Socialist Review*. In 1905 he also launched the ILP's 'Socialist Library' to introduce British readers to major international works of socialist thought. *To the promoters of this Library*, he announced,

Socialism appears to be not only the ideal which has to be grasped before the benumbing pessimism which lies upon the minds of would-be reformers can be removed, but also the one idea which is guiding such progressive legislation and administration today as are likely to be of permanent value.[47]

MacDonald may not have been a socialist in Beatrice Webb's understanding of the word. He certainly was one according to his own, and he devoted considerable energy to disseminating this conception of socialism. Even in 1931 he insisted that he remained faithful to these ideals of a lifetime, and it is worth considering how far that was true. Socialism in MacDonald's exposition had always been eclectic, combining liberal and conservative elements with socialist ones. Over the course of his career, the balance between these shifted, perhaps due to the pressure of events, perhaps because of his own changing position in society. Even before the formation of the National Government, some observers thought he seemed more of a conservative than a socialist. His conservatism, however, was not a simple denial of his socialism, but deeply rooted within it.

The basis of his political philosophy was the idea of society as a living organism. As he put it in one of his socialist treatises, the state was *an organic body in which the various organs find a place in a unified personality, and discover their liberty in that personality.*[48] It might be tempting to dismiss this as a mere residue of the Lossiemouth Field Club and MacDonald's early fascination for the natural sciences. In reality, such metaphors provided far more just than an arresting turn of phrase. Many of the mysteries of MacDonald's whole political outlook can be traced to this organicist view of society and the distinctive conception of socialism that was based upon it.[49]

First and foremost, the organic metaphor provided an alternative to any notion of competitive individualism or what he called *atomic* individualism. This, of course, was what made MacDonald a socialist. It implied the elevation of the interests of the community, however defined, over the merely private interests that currently dominated it. This was common to all forms of socialism conceived as a project of social transformation in the interests of the many. At the same time, however, the organic metaphor suggested a more distinctive accent, namely the opposition, not just to individualism, but to group or sectional interests that jeopardised the integrity of the whole. Again, there were many socialists who held that such interests would lose their significance in the socialist society of the future. But for MacDonald, the conception of society as already a living organism meant the rejection of any sectional group as the purported agent of social change. In particular, he repudiated any idea of socialism as a politics of interest representation or emancipation based on class. It was, he wrote during the war, *a movement of liberal ideas, not a combination of an industrial group*; and on this basis he repudiated Marxism, syndicalism and a narrow trade union labourism alike.[50] MacDonald was always diffident about movements like guild socialism that accorded a central role to the higher development of trade unions. He was unambiguously a state socialist who had an intrinsic preference for the state over such voluntary organisations but sectional organisations as corresponding better to his notion of society as an organic entity.

Many Conservatives have shared this profoundly organicist view of society. When MacDonald used the language of the nation rather than community, as he increasingly did in his later years, the resemblance was more obvious still. They cannot however simply be conflated. When MacDonald put himself outside the conservative nation during the war years, it was because he rejected the idea of a competitive struggle between these different states or communities. This internationalism, with all its caveats, was as basic to his political identity as the evolutionism that sometimes cut across it. For example, it can be seen both in his commitment to Indian self-determination and the cautious approach he took in respect of its achievement.

As a socialist MacDonald also had the conception of society as being constantly in a state of change, with socialism itself representing either its direction or its end-goal. Here again, much can be ascribed to the formative Darwinian outlook which was always to mark him out as a late Victorian or Edwardian. Key concepts were those of evolution and adaptation as the guarantor of social progress conceived as a matter of scientific necessity. If the idea of change distinguished him from Conservatives, the idea of adaptation distinguished from many socialists. For MacDonald, these evolutionary concepts were inherently gradualist in character. The idea of revolution, by which he was never drawn even in the abstract, struck him as merely primitive or pre-scientific. What was more problematic was the role of human agency, including the agency of government, in this unfolding of an evolutionary telos. MacDonald has sometimes been likened to the dogmatic Marxist possessing so firm a belief in economic determinism that the revolution could be expected to arrive of itself. With MacDonald it was the process of gradual social reform that seemed inherent in the very nature of society. What socialists might do to expedite that process was not always clear. What action they should take should the process judder to a halt, as for example in an economic slump, was almost never clear. Unlike many of his Labour colleagues, MacDonald did not even have a more limited discourse of group representation to fall back on. The unemployed in 1931 represented a merely sectional interest that would have to recognise the greater interest of the nation like everybody else.

A final theme that was intrinsic to this conception of society was the idea of differentiation by function, or according to the 'various organs' which made up the state's composite personality. This notion of differentiation was common in the Fabian socialism of the time. Often it was linked to a discourse of 'brains', or professional expertise – including expertise in the art of government. It was thus profoundly elitist in its possible implications. The new age of the masses was one in which elitist theories flourished and MacDonald himself was strongly influenced by writers on the crowd like Gustave Le Bon and William Trotter. It was on this ambivalence about the new mass democracy that his conceptions of representative government were founded.

The faith that the voice of the people is the voice of God is now about thirty years out of date.

MACDONALD

As early as the turn of the century he expressed disappointment in the quality of the new democracy. *The faith that the voice of the people is the voice of God is now about thirty years out of date.*[51] The experiences of the First World War, whether crowds were revolutionary or jingoistic, made him more distrustful still. His writings are peppered with misgivings about what he saw as the herd instinct, bound up with his apprehensions about the modern city. *The mass of the people are indifferent or are merely agitated*, he wrote in 1921. *Their interests are too much like a tide flowing hither and thither, obedient to every passing attractive moon. They are responsive to suggestion, and primitive in their impulses.*[52] In the shock of losing Leicester in 1918, he even made an extraordinary attack on the new women voters whom he blamed for his defeat. These were *bloodthirsty, cursing their hate, issuing from the courts and alleys crowded with children, reeking with humanity – the sad flotsam and jetsam of wild emotion.*[53] He had represented them in Parliament for 12 years.

The Baldwin-MacDonald regime

'Thus began that period of fourteen years which may well be called "The Baldwin-MacDonald Régime". At first in alternation but eventually in political brotherhood, these two statesmen governed the country. Nominally the representatives of opposing parties, of contrary doctrines, of antagonistic interests, they proved in fact to be more nearly akin in outlook, temperament and method than any other two men who had been Prime Ministers since that Office was known to the Constitution. Curiously enough, the sympathies of each extended far into the territory of the other. Ramsay MacDonald nursed many of the sentiments of the old Tory. Stanley Baldwin, apart from a manufacturer's ingrained approval of Protection, was by disposition a truer representative of mild Socialism than many to be found in the Labour ranks.'[Winston Churchill, *The Second World War* Vol 1(Cassell & Co, London: 1948) p 171.]

Biographers and historians in the Labour tradition have naturally dwelt on the consequences of these cross-party alignments for the Labour Party. Possibly the consequences for the Conservative Party were just as significant. To Labour and many of its historians, the National Government appears as a Conservative government in disguise. To Conservatives and their historians the concessions it involved were real ones, but at the same time allowed Baldwin to outmanoeuvre diehard elements to his right. 'By diluting the influence of those reactionary and doctrinaire Conservative sections which had been so troublesome to him in opposition, the coalition election [of 1931] consolidated [Baldwin's] version of a modern, permeable, and 'national' Conservatism. In the short term this included sound budgets, tolerance of high unemployment, and restricted social expenditure. But it also came to mean sterling management, cheap money, a house-building boom, agricultural marketing, industrial reorganisation and, as the economy slowly recovered, resumed social reform.' [Philip Williamson, *Stanley Baldwin. Conservative leadership and national values* (Cambridge University Press, Cambridge: 1999), pp 445.]

It was on this distrust in the capacity of the democracy that MacDonald based his ideal of the professional politician. Majoritarianism itself was only a form of sectionalism, and the mob was just its uglier side. Instead, MacDonald, with his organicist conceptions, upheld the notion of the general will of which the state was the embodiment and the statesman the interpreter. Often this might mean ignoring what the democracy actually thought it wanted. *The difference which exists between the real will and the expressed will of the individual is of the greatest importance in politics*, he wrote in 1909. *To discover it is the task of the statesman who knows how far expressed desire is not real desire, who understands how he is to speak for what is in the heart but not on the lips of the people, and who, without mandates, and even against mandates, does what the people really want.*[54]

MacDonald thus rejected all notions of direct democracy, for example in the widely canvassed proposal of the referendum. Against the *purely liberal view of democracy ... as the government of equally enlightened and capable citizens*, he set the principle of *differentiation of function* and hence of the particular function of leadership. The democratic ideal, as he put it already at the turn of the century, was *no longer the rule of the whole people, but the wise use of political power to regulate and control conditions of life which used to be regarded as beyond political concern.* The issue was not one of 'rights', but of 'authority'.[55]

'He {MacDonald} is a compound of vanity and vindictiveness. His snobbish instincts incline him to association with Tories.'

LLOYD GEORGE

By the time of the second Labour government it was becoming rather common to suggest that MacDonald would have made a good leader of the Conservative Party. H N Brailsford, a former UDC collaborator, came to that view. So did Stanley Baldwin, and he must have known something about it.[56] Political gossip centred on a possible compact between Labour and the Liberals, and the renewal of the progressive alliance to which MacDonald had once been so committed. Lloyd George for one had no hopes of such an arrangement. MacDonald, he said, simply hated the Liberals. 'He is a compound of vanity and vindictiveness. His snobbish instincts incline him to association with Tories.'[57] Like every accurate prediction, it is one that demands to be taken seriously.

Nevertheless, the snobbery was possibly symptomatic rather than a motive force. In his one significant post-war writing MacDonald described as the two great forces at work in society *habit, the force of stagnation* and *reason, the force of change*. Stagnation he rejected as merely exacerbating the impulse of upheaval. However, he also warned against an excess of reason: forgetful of tradition, forgetful of its historical inheritance, forgetful *that the material upon which change and reason have to work is that of the society into which men were born; that no generation can build ... save upon the structures which it inherited.*[58] With his apprehensions of *slavery* on the one hand, and the *mad wrath* of revolution on the other, this seems almost the perfect counterpoise to Baldwin. Baldwin recognised the need to accommodate the forces of change, and MacDonald equally so the forces of habit. *Freedom,* wrote one of them – it was actually MacDonald – *is the only guarantee of stability ... because the life of communities is one long process of adapting experience to habit and reason.* The object was stability; adaptation was the means of achieving it. It reads just like the credo of an intelligent conservative.

Taking care of the pounds

Perhaps he was also an effective conservative. As a force of habit managing forces of change, he might well bear comparison with Baldwin himself. As a force of change himself, on the other hand, MacDonald as Prime Minister was quite remarkably ineffective. An unkind assessment of Gladstone was that there was 'no great thing he did or wanted to do'.[59] An unkind assessment of MacDonald would be that there was a great thing he wanted done and he had no idea how to do it. The thing he wanted done, or said he wanted done, was the transformation of society on the altogether different and superior ethical foundations he described as socialism. But MacDonald had no real conception of how little things might bring this about. He had no proper sense of the value of little things in themselves. And he had no contingency plans to deal with problems that might crop up on the way. In a revolutionary politician these might have been weaknesses. In a reformist one they were disastrous. The view has been expressed that the failure of the second Labour government was that of a 'parliamentary party with a Utopian ethic' that was not fit for the kind of power it was called upon to exercise.[60] In relation to its leader the proposition seems unarguable.

Elements both of personal character and social philosophy contributed to MacDonald's limitations as a constructive politician. Three issues may be singled out. First, he had little idea of how to formulate realisable priorities for government and resisted pressure to do so as a constraint upon the role leadership. Secondly, he developed a style of political rhetoric which was masterly in its evasiveness and disguised through its grandiloquence the lack of any practical purchase. Thirdly, he was jealous of political rivals and consistently sought to exclude or marginalise colleagues whose competence in these matters was greater than his own.

In theory, MacDonald did not deny the need for a programme. *Bearing in mind that the watchword of Socialism is Evolution, not Revolution, and that its battlefield is Parlia-*

ment, its immediate programme becomes of the utmost importance, he wrote just before the war. The difference between the socialist politician and the non-socialist was that the socialist had a map of where they were going.[61] In 1920 MacDonald even published a version of that map entitled *A Policy for the Labour Party*. What is remarkable about it, however, is how little it provides of what might usually be regarded as a policy. Even in expounding what he called 'a programme', achievable policy objectives were spelt out in a perfunctory and abstract fashion hardly credible in one shortly to be charged with carrying them out. MacDonald instead offered his inimitable reworking of the old adage: *Take care of the pounds and the pence will take care of themselves*:

I have been taking care of the pounds. Programmes are meaningless unless in relation to some conception of Society and the State. An election address consisting of a programme is generally the least effective part of a candidate's equipment.

Extended from the candidate to the party as a whole, the disavowal of any effective notion of the mandate may be linked to his emphasis on the guiding role of the statesman. More important than programmes, to the wise elector, was the political group to which the candidate belonged and *the equipment of mind and character which he wishes to place at their disposal. Knowing these more general and fundamental things they can take the items of his programme pretty much on trust, for at best they can change with the tides of the day and their relative value is always in a state of flux*.[62] It was Baldwin in the 1920s who was consistently critical of what he regarded as the demagoguery

I have been taking care of the pounds. Programmes are meaningless unless in relation to some conception of Society and the State. An election address consisting of a programme is generally the least effective part of a candidate's equipment.

MACDONALD

of 'promises'.[63] But already in this post-war policy for the Labour Party, a taste of MacDonald's doctor's mandate of 1931 can be discerned.

In the negative sense, MacDonald was therefore assiduous in heading off any clear and precise commitments either to his party or to the electorate. Characteristically, when he moved to Frognal in 1925 he blamed his need to make a living for his inability to work out the 'constructive proposals' he thought the movement needed.[64] Nevertheless, when a year or two later the Labour Party agreed to draw up just such a 'programme of legislation and administrative action', it was MacDonald who seemed most guarded regarding both specificity and timescale. Agreed in 1928, the resulting document, *Labour and the Nation*, was much criticised for its lack of precision and offered little practical guidance to an incoming Labour government. Even R H Tawney, who drafted it, pleaded with MacDonald the following year for *'something concrete and definite* about unemployment' in Labour's election programme.[65] MacDonald, however, offered what was almost a Labourist variation on Baldwin's theme of 'Safety First': short on detail and consciously aimed at reassuring where Lloyd George spread disquiet. Fitness to govern appeared to be an object in itself.

The famous obscurity of MacDonald's prose may either have been the masterly vehicle of this ambiguity or a sign of his genuine mystification as to what he actually meant. Examples have sometimes been reproduced from his later years in office, when a tendency to opaqueness was compounded by his deteriorating eyesight and the difficulty he had in concentrating. Even in his heyday, however, the obscurity of his style excited comment. Taking the despatch box as Labour's first Foreign Secretary, he thus responded to a Liberal request to clarify the government's position on European security: *whoever is at the Foreign Office, whether I stay or whether I go, whether the Government is going to last until the first stages of these negotiations have been completed or not, whoever is responsible for the conduct of these negotiations, the negotiations must be conducted by somebody, and unless they have a very clear view of a complete policy they are not going to finish the negotiations with a settlement that is going to be the foundation for something bigger and greater and more full of hope and value to the world at large. That is the position regarding Security, so far as the Government is concerned, and so far as it can express its views at the present moment in relation to the coming negotiations ...*

'In so far as it is intelligible', Lloyd George objected, the speech was singularly unhelpful. 'I am completely at a loss, after listening with very great care ... to know what his policy is ...'[66] The style was possibly perfect for a party that did not always know what its policy was, but knew that it stood for something. It also had obvious advantages for a minority government. In assemblies like the League of Nations, where the object was to evoke common aspirations without arousing a spirit of contention, it even had a certain functionality. The tragedy for MacDonald was that on issues demanding government initiative, notably unemployment, he could not move beyond such rhetorical forms or even create the appearance of a leader bent on decisive action.

No politician has every quality of leadership. Cabinet government, or the resources of party, provide a compensation for that limitation. MacDonald's third and perhaps most fatal weakness was that he lacked the capacity to draw on these wider resources, not least as the result of his own insecurity and jealousy. Often he complained of Labour's weakness in personnel. From Hardie through to Henderson, Morel and Wheatley he showed a consistent wariness of its stronger personalities, and a no less consistent preferment of weaker vessels like Thomas or personal followers like Thomson. Snowden was the obvious exception to this. As MacDonald's peer within the labour movement and an authority on financial matters, he could not realistically be excluded from the MacDonald's cabinets. Nor did MacDonald have any idea how to stand up to him, and he was almost afraid to. Snowden reciprocated with withering contempt.

MacDonald's strength was in going beyond Labour's traditional constituency for members of his governments. The breadth of his first Cabinet has been widely remarked upon. His colleagues from the UDC certainly could not all be described as weak vessels. Nevertheless, in extending them his patronage within the framework of the labour movement, it is clear that MacDonald regarded them as in some degree his debtors. His response to the resignation from his second Cabinet of the former Liberal minister C P Trevelyan was revealing:

Some of us gave you and others, who were not acceptable to our friends at the time, a very generous welcome, and we expected great assistance.... it is curious that our greatest troubles are coming from those who were the latest converts, whose study of Socialism is the least thorough, and whose knowledge of the Movement is the least intimate ... No one knows better than you the great embarrassments which now beset us and you choose this time ... to add reflections upon general policy which I must say you, of all my colleagues, are least entitled to make.[67]

An obvious point of contrast in this respect is with Clement Attlee. Though often thought inconspicuous in himself, Attlee's great accomplishment as a Prime Minister was in successfully harnessing the energies of a formidable and potentially fractious team of ministers. He also had a large majority and a clear set of working objectives: effectiveness in government is not just down to prime ministerial aptitude. Nevertheless, MacDonald's lack of experience in any other Cabinet role showed badly in his handling of his colleagues. Though he was not a strong Prime Minister, he was singularly ill-equipped for the alternative option of effective Cabinet government.

Had MacDonald had the ability to acknowledge his short-comings they might have been better overcome. Instead, he adopted the manner of a true tragedian, in the grip of forces beyond most mortals' comprehension. Politics for MacDonald had long been an art of performance, and as the statesman laden with the cares of the world he took this almost to the point of self-parody. Visiting Chequers during the second Labour government, the Fabian socialist Margaret Cole encountered him playing three roles in a single afternoon. One was that of the inheritor of broad acres; another, more perfunctorily, that of the Son of the People; the third – at greatest length and most feelingly – that of 'the Lonely Leader grappling with problems which none but he could understand and burdened with inferior colleagues not one of whom really appreciated him or inspired his confidence'.[68] In performing this role, he retained no redeeming sense of the ridiculous. In 1928, Britain's leading trade unionist requested him as Leader of the Opposition to follow up the issue of steel quotas. *My dear Bevin*, he replied wearily: *Do you remember a tribe of Judah named Issacher which was likened to an ass upon whose shoulders innumerable burdens were heaped? I am that tribe.*[69]

My dear Bevin, do you remember a tribe of Judah named Issacher which was likened to an ass upon whose shoulders innumerable burdens were heaped? I am that tribe.

MACDONALD

Countless accounts provide a similar picture. MacDonald did not just get tired; he told you he was tired. He did not just brood on his loneliness; he liked to get it off his chest. His diaries, which must be regarded as his notes for posterity, display both self-absorption and self-dramatisation to a quite exceptional degree.

A political verdict on MacDonald might be that he was a highly skilled party strategist who lacked sufficient clarity of purpose to lead a serious reforming government. The lack of clarity is manifest. MacDonald claimed to look after the pounds; but he also took only one step at a time. It is hardly surprising that the first real step was never taken and the harvest even of pennies was so meagre. If a case is to be made for him as Prime Minister, it must be the Baldwinian one of his having steered his country through an age of extremes without succumbing to them. Whether in spirit of commendation or of indictment, the two names are hardly separable. In 1940, the anti-appeasement polemic *Guilty Men* summed up 14 years of British government this way: Baldwin, MacDonald, Baldwin, MacDonald, MacDonald-Baldwin, Baldwin-MacDonald. It did not, however, do this to flatter them. By 1940 the extremes were at the gate and stability appeared as mere complacency, unequal to the challenge of events. Baldwin's reputation took many years to recover. In many ways, MacDonald's never has.

It is in this sense that he had no posterity. In a typical Labour home of the 1920s, a portrait of MacDonald hung in the hallway. One of the children recalled her father coming home the day the National Government was formed. Disillusionment was not so much mute as beyond coherent expression. 'There's Dad in the passage, he's got the frame round his neck ... and he's standing like this: "You bloody traitor, you bloody –" tearing the picture up into little pieces ...'[70] MacDonald had done much to establish the Labour Party. One of the ironies of his career is that by his breaking with it in such dramatic fashion, he helped consolidate its collective sense of identity even as its anathema.

NOTES

Introduction: A Hybrid Ancestry

1. The document is reproduced in David Marquand, *Ramsay MacDonald* (Jonathan Cape, London: 1977).
2. Robert Skidelsky, *Politicians and the Slump. The Labour Government of 1929–1931* (Penguin, Harmondsworth: 1970 edn) p 82, hereafter Skidelsky, *Politicians*.
3. Lord Elton, *The Life of James Ramsay MacDonald* (Collins, London: 1939) pp 19–20, hereafter Elton, *Life*.
4. MacDonald to Margaret MacDonald, 21 June 1896, cited Jane Cox (ed), *A Singular Marriage. A Labour love story in letters and diaries: Ramsay and Margaret MacDonald* (Harrap, London: 1988) p 65.
5. MacDonald to Margaret MacDonald, 14 July 1896, cited Cox (ed), *A Singular Marriage*, p 91.
6. Skidelsky, *Politicians*, p 78.
7. MacDonald to Lady Londonderry, cited H Montgomery Hyde, *The Londonderrys. A family portrait* (Hamish Hamilton, London: 1979) pp 193–4.

Chapter 1: The Making of a Socialist: 1866–96

1. S V Bracher, *The Herald Book of Labour Members* (Labour Publishing Co, London: 1924) pp 112–14.
2. Marquand, *Ramsay MacDonald*, p 7.
3. Elton, *Life*, pp 16–17; L MacNeill Weir, *The Tragedy of Ramsay MacDonald* (Secker & Warburg, London: 1938) pp 2–3, hereafter MacNeill Weir, *Tragedy*.
4. J Ramsay MacDonald, *Wanderings and Excursions* (Cape, London: 1925) p 24.

5. Cited Elton, *Life*, p 34.
6. Elton, *Life*, p 44.
7. J Ramsay MacDonald, *At Home and Abroad* (Cape, London: 1936) p 44.
8. Elton, *Life*, p 59.
9. J Ramsay MacDonald, *Margaret Ethel MacDonald* (London, Swarthmore Press, 1920 edn) p 183.
10. Cited Joseph Clayton, *The Rise and Decline of Socialism in Great Britain 1884–1924* (Faber & Gywer, London: 1926) p 80.
11. Cited Cox (ed), *A Singular Marriage*, p 50.
12. MacDonald to Herbert Samuel, 16 August 1895, cited Henry Pelling, *The Origins of the Labour Party* (Oxford University Press, Oxford: 1966 edn), p 167.
13. Joseph Clayton to MacDonald, 4 August 1897, cited Cox (ed), *A Singular Marriage*, p 185.

Chapter 2: Marriage and Lincoln's Inn Fields: 1896–1900

1. MacDonald, *Margaret Ethel MacDonald*, p 12.
2. MacDonald, *Margaret Ethel MacDonald*, p 45.
3. MacDonald's unpublished novel, cited Cox (ed), *A Singular Marriage*, pp 12–13.
4. See Cox (ed), *A Singular Marriage*, pp 60–5.
5. J Bruce Glasier cited Kenneth O Morgan, *Keir Hardie: Radical and Socialist* (Weidenfeld & Nicolson, London: 1975) p 126.
6. MacDonald, *Margaret Ethel MacDonald*, pp 114–17.
7. Rowland Kenney, *Westering* (Dent, London: 1939) p 129.
8. MacDonald, *Margaret Ethel MacDonald*, p 128.
9. Margaret MacDonald to JRM, 14 August 1896, cited Cox, *A Singular Marriage*, p 116.

10. MacDonald to Margaret MacDonald, 5 September 1899, in Cox, *A Singular Marriage*, p 222.

Chapter 3: From Pressure Group to Party: 1900–14

1. In Merthyr, a two-member constituency, Hardie faced two Liberal opponents, but was informally allied with one of them. The other successful candidate was Richard Bell in Derby.
2. Cited Frank Bealey and Henry Pelling, *Labour and Politics 1900–1906. A history of the Labour Representation Committee* (Macmillan, London: 1958) p 155.
3. Marquand, *Ramsay MacDonald*, p 151.
4. Cited Marquand, *Ramsay MacDonald*, p 109.
5. J Ramsay MacDonald, *The Socialist Movement* (Williams & Norgate, 1911) pp 148–9.
6. Marquand, *Ramsay MacDonald*, p 674.
7. MacDonald to Morel, 24 September 1914, cited Martin Swartz, *The Union of Democratic Control in British Politics during the First World War* (Oxford University Press, Oxford: 1971), p 19–20, hereafter Swartz, *Union*.

Chapter 4: A Socialist at War: 1914–23

1. 'Iconoclast' (Mary Agnes Hamilton), *The Man of Tomorrow. J. Ramsay MacDonald* (Leonard Parsons, London: 1923) pp 87–134; Marquand, *Ramsay MacDonald*, Ch 10; Helen Swanwick, *Builders of Peace: being ten years' history of the Union of Democratic Control* (Swarthmore Press, London: 1924); Kenneth O Morgan, *Labour People. Leaders and lieutenants from Hardie to Kinnock*, (Oxford University Press, Oxford: 1987) p 43.

2. MacDonald Papers (John Rylands University Library of Manchester) RMD 1/3/2, draft statement, August 1914.

3. MacDonald Papers (John Rylands University Library of Manchester) RMD 1/3/6 MacDonald to Morel, 24 August 1914.

4. Philip Snowden, *An Autobiography* (Ivor Nicolson & Watson, London: 2 vols, 1934) pp 363–5.

5. Cited Swartz, *Union*, p 24.

6. MacDonald to Trevelyan, 5 August 1914, cited Swartz, *Union*, p 106.

7. Marquand, *Ramsay MacDonald*, pp 192–3.

8. Elton, *Life*, pp 282, 295; Margaret Cole (ed), *Beatrice Webb's Diaries 1912–1924* (Longmans, Green & Co, London: 1952) pp 45, 55.

9. Elton, *Life*, p 247.

Chapter 5: Moderation and Honesty: the first Labour Government, 1924

1. Snowden, *Autobiography*, p 607.

2. Harold Nicolson, *King George V. His life and reign* (London: 1952) p 384; Dominic Wring, *The Politics of Marketing the Labour Party* (Palgrave, Basingstoke: 2005) p 28.

3. *The Times*, 9 January 1924.

4. MacDonald diary, 10 December 1923, cited Marquand, *Ramsay MacDonald*, p 298.

5. Margaret Cole (ed), *Beatrice Webb's Diaries 1924–1932* (Longmans, Green & Co, London: 1956) p 20.

6. MacDonald papers (John Rylands University Library of Manchester), RMD 1/14/79, Trevelyan to MacDonald, 6 January 1924.

7. Ian Wood, *John Wheatley* (Manchester University Press, Manchester: 1990) p 119.

8. *Hansard* (1924), vol 169, col 767, 12 February 1924.

9. J Ramsay MacDonald, *A Policy for the Labour Party* (Leonard Parsons, London: 1920) pp 123–36.

10. Keith Middlemas and John Barnes, *Baldwin: a Biography* (Weidenfeld & Nicolson: London, 1969) p 268; Morgan, *Labour People*, p 48.

11. Richard Burdon Haldane, *An Autobiography* (Hodder & Stoughton, London: 1929) p 322.

12. Richard W Lyman, *The First Labour Government 1924* (Chapman & Hall, London: 1957) p 213.

13. H W Nevinson, *Last Changes, Last Chances* (Nisbet, London: 1928) p 309.

14. Marquand, *Ramsay MacDonald*, p 351.

15. Cited Marquand, *Ramsay MacDonald*, p 353.

16. Alfred Zimmern, 'The Prime Minister at Geneva', *Labour Magazine* (October 1924) pp 249–51.

17. J Ramsay MacDonald, 'Protocol and pact', *Labour Magazine* (April 1925) pp 531–4.

18. Haldane, *An Autobiography*, p 327.

19. Cole (ed), *Beatrice Webb's Diaries 1924–1932*, pp 13, 28.

20. *Hansard* 29 May 1924 (Sir Robert Horne).

21. *Hansard* 29 May 1924.

22. Lyman, *First Labour Government*, p 120; Cole (ed), *Beatrice Webb's Diaries 1924–1932*, p 20.

23. Cheryl Law, *Suffrage and Power. The women's movement 1918–1929* (Tauris, London; 2000) pp 195–8.

24. On these episodes see Marquand, *Ramsay MacDonald*, Ch 16; also *Hansard*, 5 s vol 1 cols 468–9, 22 February 1909.

Chapter 6: Rectitude of Thought, Consideration of Action: the Second Labour Government, 1929–31

1. Cole (ed), *Beatrice Webb's Diaries 1924–1932*, p 63.
2. Egon Wertheimer, *Portrait of the Labour Party* (Putnams, London: 1929) p 176, hereafter Wertheimer, *Portrait*.
3. Wertheimer, *Portrait*, pp 174–5.
4. MacNeill Weir, *Tragedy*, p 343.
5. Marquand, *Ramsay MacDonald*, p 656.
6. Skidelsky, *Politicians*, p 11.
7. Cited Marquand, *Ramsay MacDonald*, p 484.
8. MacDonald papers (John Rylands University Library of Manchester), RMD 1/4/76, MacDonald to J H Palin, 11 August 1929.
9. J M Kenworthy, *Sailors, Statesmen – and Others* (Rich & Cown, London: 1933) p 291.
10. MacDonald papers (John Rylands University Library of Manchester), RMD 1/14/16, MacDonald to Hartshorn, 19 August 1930.
11. MacDonald papers (John Rylands University Library of Manchester), MacDonald to Hartshorn 2 October and 5 December 1930, MacDonald to F W Hirst 30 December 1930.
12. Cited Marquand, *Ramsay MacDonald*, p 572.
13. Cited Andrew Thorpe, *The British General Election of 1931* (Oxford University Press, Oxford: 1991) p 89.

Chapter 7: 'The echo that was MacDonald': the MacDonald-Baldwin Governments, 1931–7

1. Cited Marquand, *Ramsay MacDonald*, p 651.
2. Marquand, *Ramsay MacDonald*, p 728.
3. Thorpe, *The British General Election of 1931*, Ch 10.
4. Again including the ILP and unendorsed candidates.
5. *Hansard* 30 March 1910, col 1366.

6. Cited Marquand, *Ramsay MacDonald*, p 723.
7. Robert Rhodes James (ed), *Memoirs of a Conservative. J C C Davidson's memoirs and papers 1910–37* (Weidenfeld & Nicolson, London: 1969) p 378.
8. Cited Robert Rhodes James, *Bob Boothby. A Portrait* (Hodder & Stoughton, London: 1991) pp 142–3.
9. Reginald Bassett, *Nineteen Thirty-One: Political Crisis* (Macmillan, London: 1958) p 355.

Chapter 8: No Possible Posterity? Ramsay MacDonald in Retrospect

1. Trevor Lloyd, 'James Ramsay MacDonald' in John P Mackintosh, *British Prime Ministers in the Twentieth Century* (Weidenfeld & Nicolson, London: 1977) p 156.
2. Wertheimer, *Portrait*, p 176.
3. Ramsay MacDonald, *Socialism and Government* (ILP, London: 2 vols, 1909), vol 1, p 124.
4. MacDonald, *At Home and Abroad*, p 11.
5. Joe Toole, *Fighting Through Life* (Rich & Cowan, London: 1935) pp 154–5.
6. *Socialist Review*, January 1923, p 26.
7. Iconoclast' (Mary Agnes Hamilton), *Fit to Govern* (Leonard Parsons, London: 1924) pp 10–11.
8. 'Iconoclast', *Man of Tomorrow*, p 62.
9. Elton, *Life*, pp 15–16.
10. J Ramsay MacDonald, 'A nook of peace' in *At Home and Abroad*, pp 21–33.
11. MacDonald, 'A nook of peace' in *At Home and Abroad*, pp 21–33.
12. J Ramsay MacDonald, *Socialism: Critical and Constructive* (Cassells, London: 1929 edn), pp 183–96.
13. MacNeill Weir, *Tragedy*, p 242.

14. Marquand, *Ramsay MacDonald*, p 247; *Hansard*, 15 May 1908, cols 1483–4.
15. MacDonald, *Socialism: Critical and Constructive*, pp 192–3.
16. *Hansard*, 22 February 1909, cols 468–9, 30 March, col 1369,
17. J Ramsay MacDonald, 'The people into power' in Stanton Coit (ed), *Ethical Democracy* (Grant Richards: London, 1900) p 65.
18. Cited D L LeMahieu, *A Culture for Democracy. Mass communication and the cultivated mind in Britain between the wars* (Oxford University Press, Oxford: 1988), p 150.
19. MacDonald, *At Home and Abroad*, p 24.
20. Thomas Jones (ed Keith Middlemas), *Whitehall Diary volume II. 1926–1930* (Oxford University Press, Oxford, 1969) p 56.
21. Cole (ed), *Beatrice Webb's Diaries 1924–1932*, pp 121–2.
22. Cole (ed), *Beatrice Webb's Diaries 1924–1932*, p 18.
23. J Ramsay MacDonald, 'Hopeman' (1913) in *Wanderings and Excursions*, pp 33–4.
24. MacDonald, *At Home and Abroad*, pp 32–3.
25. Cox (ed), *A Singular Marriage*, pp 77–8
26. Cox (ed), *A Singular Marriage*, pp 68–9.
27. Passfield papers 2/4/F/6, Beatrice Webb to Betty Balfour, 22 August 1913.
28. MacDonald Papers (John Rylands University Library of Manchester), RMD 1/14/155, MacDonald to Baldwin, 17 August 1935.
29. Joseph Clayton, *The Rise and Decline of Socialism in Great Britain*, pp 122–3.
30. Wertheimer, *Portrait*, pp 138–9, 176–7.

31. Cited David Howell, *MacDonald's Party. Labour identities and crisis* (Oxford University Press, Oxford: 2002) p 256.
32. Sheila Lochhead in Cox (ed), *A Singular Marriage*, p 379.
33. MacDonald, *Socialism: Critical and Constructive*, p 280.
34. MacDonald Papers (John Rylands University Library of Manchester), RMD 1/1/33, JRM to H Kiddle, 16 May 1894.
35. See Ross McKibbin, *The Evolution of the Labour Party 1910–1924* (Oxford University Press, Oxford: 1983 edn) pp 62–70.
36. Rowland Kenny in the *English Review*, March 1913, cited Kenny, *Westering*, p 126.
37. MacDonald, *Wanderings and Excursions*, p 116.
38. On this see Chris Howard, '"The focus of the mute hopes of a whole class", Ramsay MacDonald and Aberavon, 1922–29', *Llafur*, 7, 1 (1996), pp. 68–77; also Marquand, *Ramsay MacDonald*, pp 280–3.
39. Nevinson, *More Changes, More Chances*, pp 315–16.
40. Brown, *So Far...* (Allen & Unwin, London: 1943) p 129.
41. MacDonald, *At Home and Abroad*, pp 71–2.
42. MacDonald Papers (John Rylands University Library of Manchester), RMD 1/14/68, MacDonald to Londonderry, 16 February 1926.
43. Sidney Webb to Beatrice Webb, 28 September 1925 in Norman Mackenzie (ed), *The Letters of Sidney and Beatrice Webb* (Cambridge University Press, Cambridge: 1978) vol 3, p 246.
44. National Archives 30/69 1171 MacDonald to Mrs M Motters Porter, 13 December 1926, MacDonald to H O Coleman, 8 December 1926.

45. Cited Hyde, *The Londonderrys*, p 191.

46. Cole (ed), *Beatrice Webb's Diaries 1924–1932*, p 65.

47. Dominic Wring, *The Politics of Marketing the Labour Party*, p 26; Philip Williamson, *Stanley Baldwin: Conservative leadership and national values* (Cambridge University Press, Cambridge: 1999) p 83.

48. MacDonald, *Socialism and Government*, Vol 1, pp 178–9.

49. MacDonald, 'The people into power', p 79.

50. J Ramsay MacDonald, *Socialism After the War* (National Labour Press, Manchester: 1917) p 40.

51. MacDonald, 'The people into power', pp 60–1.

52. MacDonald, *Socialism: Critical and Constructive*, p 18.

53. Elton, *Life*, p 345.

54. MacDonald, *Socialism and Government*, Vol 1, pp 8–9.

55. MacDonald, 'The people into power', pp 75–6.

56. F M Leventhal, *The Last Dissenter. H.N. Brailsford and his world* (Oxford University Press, Oxford: 1985); Jones, *Whitehall Diary*, p 171.

57. Lloyd George papers (House of Lords Record Office) L/17/11/24, Lloyd George to C P Scott, 15 October 1927.

58. MacDonald, *Socialism: Critical and Constructive*, p 19.

59. Sir Stanley Leathes, cited 'Iconoclast', *Man of Tomorrow*, p 140.

60. Skidelsky, *Politicians*, p 12.

61. MacDonald, *Socialist Movement*, p 150.

62. MacDonald, *Policy for the Labour Party*, pp 160–1.

63. Williamson, *Stanley Baldwin*, p 158.

64. Sidney Webb to Beatrice Webb, 28 September 1925 in Norman and Jean Mackenzie (eds), *Letters of Sidney and Beatice Webb. Volume 3: 1912–1943* (Cambridge University Press, Cambridge: 1978) p 250.

65. Tawney cited Marquand, *Ramsay MacDonald*, p 484.

66. *Hansard*, 27 March 1924, cols 1605–7.
67. MacDonald papers (John Rylands University Library of Manchester) RMD 1/14/83, MacDonald to Trevelyan, 28 February 1931.
68. Margaret Cole, *The Life of G D H Cole* (Macmillan, London: 1971) p 167.
69. MacDonald papers (John Rylands University Library of Manchester), RMD 1/14/93, MacDonald to Bevin, 26 June 1928.
70. Vi Willis cited Daniel Weinbren, *Generating Socialism. Recollections of Life in the Labour Party* (Sutton, Stroud: 1997) p 86.

CHRONOLOGY

Year	Premiership

1924 22 January: James Ramsay MacDonald becomes the first Labour
Prime Minister, aged 57.

April: The Dawes Plan is published. MacDonald convenes the
London Conference that successfully achieves the settlement of
the reparations crisis.

August: Wheatley Housing Act. Two draft treaties agreed with the
Soviet Union are concluded, including controversial provisions
for a possible Soviet loan.

September: MacDonald becomes the first British Prime Minister to
address the League of Nations.

October: Geneva Protocol. Government loses vote of confidence in
the Commons.

November: The Zinoviev letter is published by the *Daily Mail* four
days before the general election. Labour loses almost a quarter
of its MPs, despite increasing their popular vote by more than a
million.

4 November: MacDonald leaves office for the first time.

1929 5 June: Ramsay MacDonald becomes the head of a Labour
government: Labour has 287 MP's compared to the Conservatives'
260 and the Liberals' 59.

August: Anglo-Egyptian Treaty.

October: MacDonald visits the United States, the first Prime
Minister to do so in an official capacity. Round Table Conference,
the Viceroy and Indian leaders discuss Dominion status.

The Wall Street Crash.

History	Culture
Death of Lenin.	Noel Coward, *The Vortex*.
Turkish national assembly expels the Ottoman dynasty.	E M Forster, *A Passage to India*.
Greece is proclaimed a republic.	Thomas Mann, *The Magic Mountain*.
Nazi party enters the Reichstag with 32 seats for the first time, after the elections to the German parliament.	George Bernard Shaw, *St Joan*.
Calvin Coolidge, Republican, wins US Presidential Election.	'The Blue Four' expressionist group is formed.
	George Braque, *Sugar Bowl*.
	Fernand Leger, *Ballet Mecanique*.
	King George V makes first royal radio broadcast, opening the British Empire Exhibition at Wembley.
Dictatorship is established in Yugoslavia under King Alexander I; constitution is suppressed.	Jean Cocteau, *Les Enfants Terribles*.
	Ernest Hemingway, *A Farewell to Arms*.
St Valentines Day Massacre of Chicago gangsters.	Erich Remarque, *All Quiet on the Western Front*.
Fascists win single-party elections in Italy.	Chagall, *Love Idyll*.
Germany accepts Young Plan at Reparations Conference in the Hague – Allies agree to evacuate the Rhineland.	Piet Mondrian, *Composition with Yellow and Blue*.
	Museum of Modern Art New York opens.
Arabs attack Jews in Palestine following dispute over Jewish use of Wailing Wall.	Heidegger, *What is Philsophy?*
	Noel Coward, *Bittersweet*.
US stock exchange collapses, world economic crisis begins. Cessation of loans to Europe.	

Year	Premiership
1930	January: MacDonald establishes an economic advisory council, comprising expert advisers to deal with rising unemployment. The Coal Mines Act sought to balance commitments over working hours with the owners' desire for quotas. Housing Act, labelled the 'Greenwood Act' encouraged mass slum clearance. January–April: The United Kingdom, France, Italy, Japan and the US sign the London Naval Treaty regulating naval expansion. October–November: British Imperial Conference held in London: the Statute of Westminster is approved. 5 October: MacDonald's friend and colleague Lord Thomson killed with 47 others when the airship *R 101* crashes in France. November: Indian Round Table Conference opens.
1931	Oswald Mosley breaks away from the Labour Party to form the New Party along fascist lines. March: The government appoints an economy committee chaired by Sir George May. It findings proposed economies of £96 million. 24 August: MacDonald forms a National Government. Britain abandons gold standard; Pound Sterling falls drastically. October: The National Government wins a comprehensive victory in the general election, with Labour winning just 52 seats.

History	Culture
Nazi politician Wilhelm Frick becomes minister in Thuringia.	T S Eliot, *Ash Wednesday*.
Nazi party in Germany gains 107 seats.	W H Auden, *Poems*.
Name of Constantinople changed to Istanbul.	Noel Coward, *Private Lives*.
Acrylic plastics are invented.	Max Beckmann, *Self-portrait with a Saxophone*.
	George Grosz, *Cold Buffet*.
	Bela Bartok, *Cantata Profana*.
	Stravinsky, *Symphony of Psalms*.
	Alfred Adler, *The Inferiority Complex*.
	E K Chambers, *William Shakespeare*.
	Film: *All Quiet on the Western Front*.
Delhi Pact between the viceroy of India and Gandhi suspends the civil disobedience campaign.	Noel Coward, *Cavalcade*.
Bankruptcy of Credit-Anstalt in Austria begins financial collapse of Central Europe.	William Faulkner, *Sanctuary*.
	Robert Frost, *Collected Poems*.
	Gershwin, *Of thee I sing*.
	George Dyson, *The Canterbury Pilgrims Oratorio*.
Nazi leader Adolf Hitler and Alfred Hugenberg of the German National Party agree to co-operate.	Salvador Dali, *The Persistence of Memory*.
Bankruptcy of German Danatbank leads to closure of all German banks.	Max Beckmann, *Still Life with Studio Window*.
	Architecture: Empire State Building New York.
	Films: *Dracula. Little Caesar*.

Year	Premiership

1932   Oswald Mosley founds the British Union of Fascists.
       January: The British government decides not to support the US
           Stimson Doctrine, which urged countries not to recognise acts
           that violate the Kellogg-Briand Pact.
       July: Anglo-French Pact of Friendship is signed in Lausanne.
       September: The Ottawa agreements saw the introduction of tariffs,
           provoking Snowden's resignation from the Cabinet.

1933   February: MacDonald's proposed cuts in troop numbers fail despite
           endorsement from the US, as negotiations collapse at the Geneva
           Disarmament Conference.
       March: The government responds to the economic crisis in
           Newfoundland by setting up a Royal Commission to investigate
           the financial state of the Empire.
       April: Anglo-German Trade Agreement.
       July: Britain, France, Germany and Italy sign a diluted version of
           Mussolini's proposed Four-Power Pact.

History	Culture
Gandhi returns to India and is later arrested.	Brecht, *St Joan of the Slaughterhouses*.
Germany's Chancellor Brüning declares they cannot and will not resume reparation payments.	Aldous Huxley, *Brave New World*.
	Pablo Picasso, *Head of a Woman*.
Germany withdraws temporarily from the Geneva Disarmament Conference, demanding permission for armaments equal to those of other powers.	Alexander Calder exhibits *Stabiles and Mobiles*.
	Samuel Barber, *Overture to School for Scandal*.
F D Roosevelt wins US Presidential election in Democrat landslide.	Sergei Prokofiev, *Piano Concerto No.5 in G major Op. 55*.
Kurt von Schleicher forms ministry in Germany attempting to conciliate Centre and Left.	King George V broadcasts first Royal Christmas Day message on BBC radio.
Britain, France, Germany and Italy make the 'No Force Declaration', renouncing the use of force for settling differences.	Films: *Grand Hotel. Tarzan the Ape Man*.
Kurt von Schleicher's ministry falls.	Books by non-Nazi and Jewish authors burned in Germany.
Adolf Hitler is appointed Chancellor of Germany.	Andre Malraux, *La condition humaine*.
Fire destroys the Reichstag in Berlin.	George Orwell, *Down and Out in Paris and London*.
In Germany, the Enabling Act gives Hitler dictatorial powers.	Matisse, *The Dance*.
Japan announces it will leave the League of Nations.	All modernist German art suppressed in favour of superficial realism.
Start of official persecution of Jews in Germany.	Richard Strauss, *Arabella*.
Oath of Allegiance to the British Crown is removed from Irish Constitution.	Duke Ellington's Orchestra debuts in Britain.
In Germany, suppression of all political parties other than Nazi Party.	Films: *Duck Soup. King Kong. Queen Christina*.
Germany withdraws from League of Nations and Disarmament Conference.	
Germany opens concentration camps for enemies of the Nazi regime.	

Year	Premiership
1934	February: Anglo-Russian Trade Agreement.
	Road Traffic Act introduces driving tests.
	Depressed Areas Bill introduced.
1935	January: Despite a ongoing tariff war, Britain and Ireland negotiate, and sign, the Coal-Cattle Pact to promote trade.
	February: British and French governments meet in London to discuss German rearmament.
	March: The British government announces an expansion and modernisation of national defences, focusing on the Royal Navy.
	April: Stresa Conference
	King George V's Silver Jubilee.
	7 June: Ramsay MacDonald leaves office, after heading three governments for all together six years and 289 days.

History	Culture
General strike staged in France.	F Scott Fitzgerald, *Tender Is the Night*.
Germany, 'Night of the Long Knives'.	
After German President Hindenburg dies, role of President and Chancellor are merged and Hitler becomes *Führer*.	Robert Graves, *I, Claudius*.
	Shostakovich, *Lady Macbeth of Mtsensk*.
USSR admitted to League of Nations.	Rakhmaninov, *Rhapsody on a theme of Paganini*.
In USSR, Kirov, the fourth highest communist leader, is assassinated.	Jean Cocteau, *La Machine Infernale*.
Japan renounces Washington treaties of 1922 and 1930.	Salvador Dali, *William Tell*.
	John Dewey, *Art as Experience*.
	Films: *David Copperfield*.
Anglo-Indian trade pact signed.	Karl Barth, *Credo*.
Saarland is incorporated into Germany following a plebiscite.	*Brockhaus Encyclopaedia* completed.
	George Gershwin, *Porgy and Bess*.
Germany reintroduces conscription.	Richard Strauss, *Die Schweigsame Frau*.
	T S Eliot, *Murder in the Cathedral*.
	Emlyn Williams, *Night Must Fall*.
	Ivy Compton-Burnett, *A House and its Head*.
	Films: *The 39 Steps. Top Hat*.

FURTHER READING

Compared to most of his Labour contemporaries, biographical sources for MacDonald are rich and varied. Remaining in office almost until his death, he left no memoirs unless one counts his revealing tribute to his wife: *Margaret Ethel MacDonald. A memoir* (Swarthmore Press, London: 1920). However, a number of biographies by contemporaries give a vivid sense of the strong feelings he provoked. 'Iconoclast' (Mary Agnes Hamilton), *The Man of Tomorrow. J. Ramsay MacDonald* (Leonard Parsons, London: 1923) gives a good idea of how MacDonald at his height could sweep a young female Labour journalist off her feet. Apparently Hamilton had some hope of marrying him: the dashing of these hopes might explain the cooler tone of Hamilton's sequel covering MacDonald's first year in office, *J. Ramsay MacDonald (1923–1925)* (Leonard Parsons, London: 1925). H Hessell Tiltman, *Ramsay MacDonald: Labour's Man of Destiny* (1929) is another favourable journalistic account. Lord Elton, *The Life of James Ramsay MacDonald (1866–1919)* (Collins, London: 1939) is a more substantial work by a family friend and National Labour peer. It remains an important source for his early years. For the backlash against MacDonald after 1931, there is also a trenchant account by his former parliamentary private secretary dwelling on MacDonald's consuming ambition: L MacNeill Weir, *The Tragedy of Ramsay MacDonald. A political biography* (Secker & Warburg, London: 1938). Its author's obvious grudge against MacDonald should not lead to it being so readily dismissed as has sometimes been the case.

There was a long wait for a more academic treatment. C L

Mowat even claimed in 1971 that MacDonald had suffered from 'an oblivion unparalleled among the Prime Ministers of the twentieth century'. Mowat himself attempted to redress that in his 'Ramsay MacDonald and the Labour Party' in Asa Briggs and John Saville (eds), *Essays in Labour History 1886–1923* (Macmillan, London: 1971). Six years later there at least appeared a biographical study on the grand scale that MacDonald merited: David Marquand, *Ramsay MacDonald* (Jonathan Cape, London: 1977). Drawing for the first time on MacDonald's diaries and personal papers, now accessible in the National Archives, Marquand's was a work at once of tremendous scholarship and eloquent advocacy. Seeking to rescue its subject from the obloquy and condescension of the labour movement, Marquand depicted MacDonald as perhaps the master strategist of the Labour alliance and as a politician of consistent intelligence and integrity. A sign of his achievement is that a punchier treatment like Austen Morgan, *Ramsay MacDonald* (Manchester University Press, Manchester: 1987) does not really break new ground factually. On the other hand, Morgan is critical of many aspects of MacDonald's career, including his decision to form the National Government, on which Marquand is possibly generous to a fault.

Among other biographical materials, an essay which stands out for its clarity and insight is: Trevor Lloyd, 'James Ramsay MacDonald' in John P Mackintosh, *British Prime Ministers in the Twentieth Century* (Weidenfeld & Nicolson, London: 1977). For those interested in the interface between the personal and the political, there is a fascinating scrapbook of documents: Jane Cox (ed), *A Singular Marriage. A Labour love story in letters and diaries: Ramsay and Margaret MacDonald* (Harraps, London: 1988). For the aristocratic connection, there is a chapter in H Montgomery Hyde, *The Londonderrys. A family portrait* (Hamish Hamilton, London: 1979). Constituency relations are covered in two studies: Bill Lancaster, *Radicalism, Cooperation and Socialism. Leicester working-class politics 1860–1906* (Leicester University Press, Leicester: 1987); and Chris Howard, "'The focus of the mute hopes of a whole class", Ramsay MacDonald and Aberavon, 1922–29', *Llafur*, 7 (1996) pp 68–77. The Seaham connection apparently still awaits a study.

Despite the suggestion of oblivion, several Labour history texts dating from as far back as the 1950s deal with the different phases of MacDonald's career. Already MacDonald has a bit part in Henry Pelling, *The Origins of the Labour Party* (Oxford University Press, Oxford: 1966 edn). He then figures as a major player in its sequel: Frank Bealey and Henry Pelling, *Labour and Politics 1900–1906. A history of the Labour Representation Committee* (Macmillan, London: 1958). Other important accounts of these formative years are: David Howell, *British Workers and the Independent Labour Party 1888–1906* (Manchester University Press, Manchester: 1983); Ross McKibbin, *The Evolution of the Labour Party, 1910–1924* (Oxford University Press, Oxford: 1983 edn); and Duncan Tanner, *Political Change and the Labour Party 1900–1918* (Cambridge University Press, Cambridge: 1990).

For the war years and MacDonald's Liberal contacts useful accounts are: Martin Swartz, *The Union of Democratic Control in British Politics during the First World War* (Oxford University Press, Oxford: 1971); Catherine Cline, *Recruits to Labour. The British Labour Party 1914–1931* (Syracuse University Press, Syracuse: 1963). Taking the story into the 1920s is David Howell, *MacDonald's Party. Labour identities and crisis* (Oxford University Press, Oxford: 2002). Kevin Morgan, *Labour Legends and Russian Gold* (Lawrence & Wishart, London: 2006) discusses the changing character of the Parliamentary Labour Party.

For MacDonald's governments, the coverage is uneven. For the first of them, there is still nothing to replace the rather pedestrian Richard W Lyman, *The First Labour Government 1924* (Chapman & Hall, London: 1957). However, the second Labour government has attracted attention as epitomising key problems of governance, party competition and economic management between the wars. An influential interpretation of the government's economic policy is Robert Skidelsky, *Politicians and the Slump. The Labour government of 1929–1931* (Macmillan, London: 1967). David Carlton, *MacDonald versus Henderson. The foreign policy of the second Labour government* (Macmillan, London: 1970) comes down rather on Henderson's side than MacDonald's. Important accounts of party politics in this period are Andrew Thorpe, *The British General Election of 1931* (Oxford University Press, Oxford: 1991) and Neil Riddell, *Labour in Crisis. The second Labour government 1929–1931* (Manchester University Press, Manchester: 1999).

MacDonald does not figure much in histories of British socialist thought – perhaps not enough. He is, for example, overlooked except in passing in J M Winter, *Socialism and the Challenge of War. Ideas and politics in Britain 1912–1918* (Routledge & Kegan Paul, London: 1974). Rodney Barker has however produced a useful short study: 'Socialism and progressivism in the political thought of Ramsay MacDonald', A J A Morris (ed), *Edwardian Radicalism 1900–1914* (Routledge & Kegan Paul, London: 1974). Less a commentary than a compendium, drawing extensively on MacDonald's journalism as well as major writings, is Benjamin Sacks, *J. Ramsay MacDonald: in thought and action* (University of New Mexico Press, Albuquerque, New Mexico: 1952).

Given the great number of Labour Party histories and biographies, it would be invidious to pick out more general treatments of these events. Three contemporary observers must suffice as having had a particular influence on received images of MacDonald. Of his colleagues, Philip Snowden provides a jaundiced view that malicious minds will read with enjoyment: *An Autobiography* (Nicholson & Watson, London: 2 vols, 1934). Beatrice Webb's diaries are more penetrating and just as acerbic; here I have drawn on the first published selections: Margaret Cole (ed), *Beatrice Webb's Diaries 1912–1924* and *Beatrice Webb's Diaries 1924–1932* (Longmans, Green & Co, London: 1952 and 1956). Finally, there is the account of the London correspondent of the German SPD, Egon Wertheimer, *Portrait of the Labour Party* (Putnams, London: 1929). Though hard to get hold of, this is immensely readable and remains one of the most penetrating accounts written of the inter-war Labour Party.

The present account draws on contemporary printed materials, including *Hansard*, and a collection of MacDonald's papers held by the University of Manchester Library. Limited use has also been made of his papers in the National Archives. I have also relied constantly on Marquand's biography without always agreeing with it. It is a pleasure to record that debt here.

PICTURE SOURCES

Page vi
Ramsay Macdonald's winning smile, photographed at
Seaham Harbour, Durham, after his election victory, 15
March 1929. (Courtesy Topham Picturepoint)

Pages 38–9
The National Government took over from Labour in 1931
under the Labour leader James Ramsay Macdonald. Despite
the boast of the 1935 election poster, the revival owed little
to government policies. The fact was that world prices were
running in Britain's favour. (Courtesy Topham Picturepoint)

Page 122
On a visit to Italy to sign the Four Power Pact in 1933,
Ramsay Macdonald is greeted by Benito Mussolini.
(Courtesy akg Images)

INDEX

A

Anderson, Sir John 68
Asquith, Herbert Henry 28, 43, 55
Atlee, Clement 41–2, 63, 118–19

B

Baldwin, Stanley 42–3, 50, 78–9, 81, 83, 86, 111, 113, 120
Bevin, Ernest 7–8
Bonar Law, Andrew 77
Bottomley, Horatio 36
Brocklehurst, Fred 19
Buxton, Noel 46

C

Callaghan, James 41–2, 83
Chamberlain, Neville 72, 78–9
Chelmsford, Viscount 50
Churchill, Winston 43, 84
Clayton, Joe 96
Clynes, J R 37, 63, 80
Cole, Margaret 119

D

Dollan, Patrick 97

E

Eden, Anthony 85

G

Gissing, George 10, 14, 15
Gladstone, Herbert 25
Gladstone, Margaret Ethel *see* Margaret MacDonald 15, 17, 18, 19
Gladstone, John 16
Gladstone, William 97
Glasier, John Bruce 16, 29
Grey, Sir Edward 30

H

Haldane, Richard (1st Viscount Haldane) 50, 55
Hamilton, Molly 31–2, 101
Hardie, James Keir 1, 11, 12, 17, 19, 23, 25, 26, 28, 32, 35, 87, 97, 100
Hartshorn, Vernon 68–9

THE 20 BRITISH PRIME MINISTERS
OF THE 20TH CENTURY

SALISBURY
Conservative politician, prime minister
1885–6, 1886–92 and 1895–1902, and
the last to hold that office in the House
of Lords.
by Eric Midwinter
Visiting Professor of Education at
Exeter University
ISBN 1-904950-54-X (pb)

BALFOUR
Balfour wrote that Britain favoured 'the
establishment in Palestine of a national
home for the Jewish people', the so-
called 'Balfour Declaration'.
by Ewen Green
of Magdalen College Oxford
ISBN 1-904950-55-8 (pb)

CAMPBELL-BANNERMAN
Liberal Prime Minister, who started the
battle with the Conservative-dominated
House of Lords.
by Lord Hattersley
former Deputy Leader of the Labour
Party and Cabinet member in Wilson
and Callaghan's governments.
ISBN 1-904950-56-6 (pb)

Asquith

ASQUITH

His administration laid the foundation of Britain's welfare state, but he was plunged into a major power struggle with the House of Lords.

by Stephen Bates

a senior correspondent for the *Guardian*.

ISBN 1-904950-57-4 (pb)

Lloyd George

LLOYD GEORGE

By the end of 1916 there was discontent with Asquith's management of the war, and Lloyd George schemed secretly with the Conservatives in the coalition government to take his place.

by Hugh Purcell

television documentary maker.

ISBN 1-904950-58-2 (pb)

Bonar Law

BONAR LAW

In 1922 he was the moving spirit in the stormy meeting of Conservative MPs which ended the coalition, created the 1922 Committee and reinstated him as leader.

by Andrew Taylor

Professor of Politics at the University of Sheffield.

ISBN 1-904950-59-0 (pb)

Baldwin

BALDWIN

Baldwin's terms of office included two major political crises, the General Strike and the Abdication.

by Anne Perkins

a journalist, working mostly for the *Guardian*, as well as a historian of the British labour movement.

ISBN 1-904950-60-4 (pb)

MacDonald

Chamberlain

Churchill

Attlee

MACDONALD

In 1900 he was the first secretary of the newly formed Labour Representation Committee (the original name for the Labour party). Four years later he became the first Labour prime minister.

by Kevin Morgan

who teaches government and politics at Manchester University.
ISBN 1-904950-61-2 (pb)

CHAMBERLAIN

His name will forever be linked to the policy of appeasement and the Munich agreement he reached with Hitler.

by Graham Macklin

manager of the research service at the National Archives.
ISBN 1-904950-62-0 (pb)

CHURCHILL

Perhaps the most determined and inspirational war leader in Britain's history.

by Chris Wrigley

who has written about David Lloyd George, Arthur Henderson and W E Gladstone.
ISBN 1-904950-63-9 (pb)

ATTLEE

His post-war government enacted a broad programme of socialist legislation in spite of conditions of austerity. His legacy: the National Health Service.

by David Howell

Professor of Politics at the University of York and an expert in Labour's history.
ISBN 1-904950-64-7 (pb)

Eden

Macmillan

Douglas-Home

Wilson

EDEN

His premiership will forever be linked to the fateful Suez Crisis.

by Peter Wilby

former editor of the *New Statesman*.

ISBN 1-904950-65-5 (pb)

MACMILLAN

He repaired the rift between the USA and Britain created by Suez and secured for Britain co-operation on issues of nuclear defence, but entry into the EEC was vetoed by de Gaulle in 1963.

by Francis Beckett

author of **BEVAN**, published by Haus in 2004.

ISBN 1-904950-66-3 (pb)

DOUGLAS-HOME

Conservative politician and prime minister 1963-4, with a complex career between the two Houses of Parliament.

by David Dutton

who teaches History at Liverpool University.

ISBN 1-904950-67-1 (pb)

WILSON

He held out the promise progress, of 'the Britain that is going to be forged in the white heat of this revolution'. The forced devaluation of the pound in 1967 frustrated the fulfilment of his promises.

by Paul Routledge

The *Daily Mirror's* chief political commentator.

ISBN 1-904950-68-X (pb)

Heath

HEATH
A passionate European, he succeeded during his premiership in effecting Britain's entry to the EC.
by Denis MacShane
Minister for Europe in Tony Blair's first government.
ISBN 1-904950-69-8 (pb)

Callaghan

CALLAGHAN
His term in office was dominated by industrial unrest, culminating in the 'Winter of Discontent'.
by Harry Conroy
When James Callaghan was Prime Minister, Conroy was the Labour Party's press officer in Scotland, and he is now editor of the Scottish *Catholic Observer.*
ISBN 1-904950-70-1 (pb)

Thatcher

THATCHER
Britain's first woman prime minister and the longest serving head of government in the 20th century (1979–90), but also the only one to be removed from office in peacetime by pressure from within her own party.
by Clare Beckett
teaches social policy at Bradford University.
ISBN 1-904950-71-X (pb)

Major

MAJOR
He enjoyed great popularity in his early months as prime minister, as he seemed more caring than his iron predecessor, but by the end of 1992 nothing seemed to go right.
by Robert Taylor
is Research Associate at the LSE's Centre for Economic Performance.
ISBN 1-904950-72-8 (pb)

Blair

BLAIR
He is therefore the last prime minister of the 20th century and one of the most controversial ones, being frequently accused of abandoning cabinet government and introducing a presidential style of leadership.
by Mick Temple
is a senior lecturer in Politics and Journalism at Staffordshire University.
ISBN 1-904950-73-6 (pb)

THE 20 BRITISH PRIME MINISTERS
OF THE 20TH CENTURY

www.hauspublishing.co.uk